General Education in Two-Year Colleges

B. Lamar Johnson, *Editor*

NEW DIRECTIONS FOR COMMUNITY COLLEGES
Sponsored by the **ERIC** Clearinghouse for Junior Colleges
ARTHUR M. COHEN, *Editor-in-Chief*
FLORENCE B. BRAWER, *Associate Editor*

Number 40, December 1982

Paperback sourcebooks in
The Jossey-Bass Higher Education Series

Jossey-Bass Inc., Publishers
San Francisco • Washington • London

EDUCATIONAL RESOURCES INFORMATION CENTER

Clearinghouse For Junior Colleges

UNIVERSITY OF CALIFORNIA, LOS ANGELES

General Education in Two-Year Colleges
Volume X, Number 4, December 1982
        B. Lamar Johnson, *Editor*

New Directions for Community Colleges Series
Arthur M. Cohen, *Editor-in-Chief*; Florence B. Brawer, *Associate Editor*

New Directions for Community Colleges (publication number USPS 121-710)
is published quarterly by Jossey-Bass Inc., Publishers, in association with
the ERIC Clearinghouse for Junior Colleges. *New Directions* is numbered
sequentially—please order extra copies by sequential number. The volume
and issue numbers above are included for the convenience of libraries.
Second-class postage rates paid at San Francisco, California, and at additional
mailing offices.

The material in this publication was prepared pursuant to a contract with
the National Institute of Education, U.S. Department of Health, Education,
and Welfare. Contractors undertaking such projects under government
sponsorship are encouraged to express freely their judgment in professional
and technical matters. Prior to publication, the manuscript was submitted
to the Center for the Study of Community Colleges for critical review and
determination of professional competence. This publication has met such
standards. Points of view or opinions, however, do not necessarily represent
the official view or opinions of the Center for the Study of Community
Colleges or the National Institute of Education.

Correspondence:
Subscriptions, single-issue orders, change of address notices, undelivered
copies, and other correspondence should be sent to *New Directions*
Subscriptions, Jossey-Bass Inc., Publishers, 433 California Street,
San Francisco, California 94104.

Editorial correspondence should be sent to the Editor-in-Chief,
Arthur M. Cohen, at the ERIC Clearinghouse for Junior Colleges,
University of California, Los Angeles, California 90024.

Library of Congress Catalogue Card Number LC 81-48568

International Standard Serial Number ISSN 0194-3081

International Standard Book Number ISBN 87589-886-6

Cover art by Willi Baum
Manufactured in the United States of America

 This publication was prepared with funding from the National Institute of
Education, U.S. Department of Health, Education, and Welfare under
contract no. 400-78-0038. The opinions expressed in the report do not
necessarily reflect the positions or policies of NIE or HEW.

Contents

Editor's Notes

General education is currently a "hot topic" in American higher education. Between 1970 and 1979, the number of scholarly articles on the subject doubled, and there has been an increasing number of books, conferences, meetings, and workshops on the topic of general education planning at institutions. Yet Mayhew (1960) pointed out that "general education is really a meaningless term since people define it in about any way their fancies dictate" (p. 9).

More recently, Boyer and Levine (1981) and Cohen and Brawer (1982) have echoed the problem noted by Mayhew. Boyer and Levine graphically suggest that "general education is the spare room of academia with no one responsible for its oversight and everyone permitted to use it as he will" (p. 3). Cohen and Brawer succinctly assert, "A good part of the difficulty with general education rests with its definition" (p. 316).

There have been a variety of definitions of general education. These are reflected in the following summary by Johnson (1952):

> General education has been described as "that education which leads to an understanding of the major fields of knowledge and the interrelationships between them,". . . as simply "the nonspecialized and nonvocational education which should be the heritage of all,". . . as "education for the common life," as an education "educating a man's humanity rather than indulging his individuality," and as "that form of education which prepares people for their common activities as citizens in a free society." Some definitions stress fields of learning and their relationships. Some see it as a core of absolutes to be found in the "Great Books." Some emphasize the common needs and activities of students — some the needs of society and the demands it places on all citizens. Others recognize both the characteristics of students and of society. Some regard general education as a process of learning, others as a combination of content and process. Some think of it as a means of developing the whole personality and conditioning its behavior. From the diversity of these and other descriptions and definitions emerges, however, a search for unity, for synthesis, a recognition of common needs and opportunities (p. 19).

1

In this volume, the writers have adopted no official definition of general education, but present varied concepts that reflect "a search for unity, for synthesis, a recognition of common needs and opportunities."

In the first chapter, the editor reviews the report of the 1952 California Study of General Education in the Junior College and emphasizes "general education in action" and the relevance of the past to the present. General education developments in 1952 that may have applicability in the present are explored.

Next, Patricia Cross views what has happened in general education in the years since 1952 and suggests that reform movements in general education seem to appear about every thirty years.

Melvin L. Barlow notes the value of both vocational and general education and makes suggestions for achieving a close and effective relationship between them.

Suanne and John Roueche report vast numbers of skill-deficient community college students and suggest what can and must be done if these students are to become generally educated.

In his chapter, Ervin L. Harlacher reports the genesis of community-based general education and points out its encasement under the umbrella of lifelong learning and describes a variety of examples of effective community general education.

Maxwell King and Seymour Fersh point out the responsibility community colleges have for international/general education. This chapter features a report on an extensive program at Brevard Community College.

Terry O'Banion and Ruth G. Shaw identify and discuss obstacles to general education and make suggestions for coping with them.

Judith S. Eaton suggests ways to advance general education through the use of institutional goals, faculty, curriculum, academic standards, and management.

A number of writers make suggestions for launching and developing programs of general education. Jeffrey Lukenbill and Robert McCabe, however, focus directly and specifically on getting started, recounting their experiences in planning and launching the general education program at Miami–Dade Community College.

Leslie Koltai emphasizes both the quantitative and the qualitative decline of education for transfer and recommends plans for revitalizing the education transfer function of the community college.

In the concluding chapter, James Palmer summarizes the literature available for further study of general education in the community college.

B. Lamar Johnson
Editor

References

Boyer, E. L., and Levine, A. *A Quest for Common Learning.* Washington, D.C.: The Carnegie Foundation for the Advancement of Teaching, 1981.

Cohen, A. M., and Brawer, F. B. *The American Community College.* San Francisco: Jossey-Bass, 1982.

Johnson, B. L. *General Education in Action.* Washington, D.C.: American Council on Education, 1952.

Mayhew, L. B. (Ed.). *General Education: An Account and an Appraisal.* New York: Harper & Row, 1960.

B. Lamar Johnson is professor of higher education, emeritus, at the University of California, Los Angeles, and distinguished professor of higher education at Pepperdine University.

"It is interesting that the issues you were addressing at that time [in General Education in Action, *published in 1952] are so relevant and timely today" (Goodlad, 1981).*

"General Education in Action": Revisited After Thirty Years

B. Lamar Johnson

The California Study of General Education in the Junior College, *General Education in Action* (Johnson, 1952), reflects views, conditions, and developments that are as timely in 1982 as they were in 1952. In this chapter, general education as viewed and reported in California junior colleges thirty years ago will be discussed under the following headings: "Why General Education Today?"; "Approaches to General Education"; and "Recommended General Education Practices in Action."

Why General Education Today?

During the California Study of General Education in the Junior College, I (as director of the study) received the following postcard query from a junior college instructor: "In a time of advanced technology, when specialized training is necessary for national survival and individual employment, why are you expending energy on the nebulous whimsy of general education?" (Johnson, 1952, p. 3).

Because of the importance of the question and because of the obvious sincerity of the writer, I wrote a letter replying to him at some length, in part as follows (Johnson, 1952):

B. L. Johnson, (Ed.). *New Directions for Community Colleges: General Education in Two-Year Colleges*, no. 40. San Francisco: Jossey-Bass, December 1982.

I fully agree with your premise that this is a time of advanced technology when specialized training is necessary for national survival and individual employment. . . .

But even competence on the job calls for more than vocational skill. . . . It is almost trite, though I think necessary, to say that our advances in technology have far outrun our advances in human relations. . . . The values that we cannot weigh, count, or measure must continue to become more and more important in our lives. While we train more and better workers, education must see to it that these workers raise the level of their citizenship. These workers and their interests are all a part of the stuff of life, of our American life.

It is these people and their nonvocational activities and interests that are the major concern of general education. For life is bigger than jobs. Workers go home. They raise families, they buy goods, they vote, they belong to churches and clubs, maintain unions, read, play, listen to radios, follow hobbies, visit friends, pray and hope and strive [p. 4].

The importance of the question raised by the instructor was "by no means limited to California, nor indeed to educators. . . . The ultimate answer must express the credo of the layman as well as of the educator, must take into account problems of local, state, national, and international consequence" (Johnson, 1952, p. 5).

With this in mind, I sent the instructor's question to selected educators and leaders of thought throughout the nation. "Eighty-two answers from university presidents, labor leaders, college instructors, editors, practicing psychiatrists, industrialists, authors, and others were unanimous in emphasizing the importance of general education today. 'The question is almost like asking, Why do we need houses, schools, and churches in an age when we have factories?' comments former President Alvin C. Eurich of the State University of New York" (Johnson, 1952, p. 6).

The following quotations summarize the respondents' endorsement of general education. Pearl Buck, for example, pointed to history as she wrote, "History proves that the superior civilization always conquers, whether or not it wins the military war" (Johnson, 1952, p. 6). Howard Mumford Jones of Harvard University asked, "Why survive merely as a technologist?" (Johnson, 1952, p. 7).

President L. A. DuBridge of the California Institute of Technology noted the importance of both general and specialized education as he pointed out "That the whole trend of specialized and professional education during recent years has been to build a sound intellectual, professional education on the basis of a broad, liberal, or general education" (Johnson, 1952, pp. 14–15). In a similar vein, Frederick L. Allen, editor of *Harper's Magazine,* asserted, "It is one of the delusions of our time that the specialist is tops, even if he is otherwise an ignoramus" (Johnson, 1952, p. 9).

Walter Reuther, national labor leader, responded that "education must do more than train competent doctors, competent engineers, and competent technicians. Education must essentially facilitate the growth of the individual and develop good people who will in turn be good doctors, good engineers, and good technicians. The development of competent technicians is infinitely less important than the development of good people. This is the purpose of general education" (Johnson, 1952, p. 12).

Roy E. Larsen, president of Time, Incorporated, also provided a definition of general education: "All of our citizens today should have free and equal access to an education which broadens the horizons of the mind, gives knowledge of the ways of men and of history, and furnishes a basis for the individual to choose his way of life and how he wants to live it. This is general education" (Johnson, 1952, pp. 11–12).

William C. Menninger, psychiatrist, suggested that the answer to the question "is a matter of mental health of the individual because in the long run he simply has to have more than bread and water" (Johnson, 1952, p. 12). Similarly, Eleanor Roosevelt had in mind the values of the human personality and of individual development as she wrote that "the type of education you mention simply trains people to earn a living or gives some special knowledge. The real value of an education is to give an all-around ability to learn, the power to think and to enjoy so that people do not live on a treadmill or wear blinders all of their lives" (Johnson, 1952, p. 13).

Finally, summarizing the importance of general education for individual development, Paul Hoffman wrote, "I hold the deep conviction that an individual with specialized training but without general education is like a tree with branches but without roots" (Johnson, 1952, p. 13).

Approaches to General Education

Clearly, general education was essentially important in 1952, just as it is in 1982. A second question, then, can be raised: How can the goals of general education be achieved?

In 1952 I noted that there was general agreement regarding the goals of general education, but that there were sharp differences among educators as to the best means of achieving these objectives. As I noted in *General Education in Action* (1952, pp. 42–46), at least six different approaches to general education were defended and urged in the early 1950s:

"1. *The 'Great Books'*

"One group represented by Hutchins, Van Doren, Foerster, and Adler advocates the 'great books' as *the* approach to general education. Proponents of this plan hold that, by studying the greatest books of ages past, students will become acquainted with the process and results of man's best thinking and will then be able to apply the resultant learning to current and future problems of day-to-day living. . .

"2. *Liberal Arts*

"A second group of educators recommends a sampling from many fields of knowledge. This is ordinarily referred to as the liberal arts approach to general education. Under this plan students are expected to take a course in English composition and at least one course in each of the major fields of learning: science, history and the social sciences, and the humanities. . .

"3. *Survey of Fields of Knowledge*

"A third approach to general education is the selection of subject-matter content on the basis of a survey of one or several allied broad fields of knowledge. Under this plan students are expected to take several survey courses plus selected electives in fields of their choice. Proponents of the survey plan hold that this particular type of course aids students to organize and synthesize thinking into large and integrated wholes. They further argue that acquaintance with broad fields of learning expands students' understandings and insights so that they may later be able to make almost daily application. . .

"4. *Functional Courses*

"A fourth approach to general education is through courses based directly upon problems and areas of living derived from and identified by studies of the characteristics and needs of students and of the society in which they live and of which they are a part. . .

"5. *Infusion Approach*

"Some educators advocate achieving general education objectives through varied courses and activities, the primary purpose of which may not be general education. Under this plan it is held that outcomes in such areas as human relations, personal adjustment, citizenship, and communication skills can be taught as opportunity arises in any area of the college program. The infusion approach is widely reported in California junior colleges. . .

"6. *Composite of Approaches*

"It is clear, of course, that the five patterns of courses here discussed may be described oversimply. Actually, most colleges do not consistently follow any single pattern. A considerable number that adhere to the liberal arts pattern also, for example, offer courses of the functional type, such as family life education, communications, and personal and social adjustment. Some of these same institutions may also offer one or more survey courses and perhaps one in the 'great books' as well. These various patterns of approaches to general education have been outlined here to suggest some of the directions of thinking and planning being carried on in general education" (pp. 42–46).

Recommended General Education Practices in Action

In planning and developing programs of general education, junior colleges need to select a "course pattern." It is also, however, necessary to plan and select — within the course pattern — programs and practices designed to achieve the objectives of general education. A major part of *General Education in Action* (some three hundred pages) is given over to reports on and descriptions of "recommended practices in action." These recommended practices fell under the following course patterns: communication skills, psychology and personal adjustment, family life education, citizenship and social studies, and humanities and the creative arts.

Also included in the California Study of General Education in the Junior College were the areas of health and physical education, the natural sciences and mathematics, vocational courses, and the extra-class program.

Conditions and viewpoints reported in this chapter emphasize the importance of and the need for general education; the general education practices reported by California junior colleges thirty years ago clearly have implications for action in community colleges today.

References

Goodlad, J. I. Memorandum to B. Lamar Johnson, June 23, 1981. Graduate School of Education, University of California, Los Angeles.

Johnson, B. L. *General Education in Action*. Washington, D.C.: American Council on Education, 1952.

B. Lamar Johnson is professor of higher education, emeritus, at the University of California, Los Angeles, and distinguished professor of higher education at Pepperdine University.

*What has happened in the thirty years that have passed
since the first major study of general education
in the community colleges?*

Thirty Years Have Passed:
Trends in General Education

K. Patricia Cross

Thirty years have passed since B. Lamar Johnson (1952) conducted his
study of the state of general education in the community colleges of California. In those thirty years, community colleges have grown from 597
colleges serving 10 percent of the undergraduates of the nation to more
than 1,200 colleges with 40 percent of the college enrollment. For community colleges, there have been ups and downs over the decades, but
by and large the movement has been upward and onward with the task
of implementing the national social priority of equal educational opportunity.

The "people's college" is indeed the rallying cry, and, while it is
sometimes hard to know what "the people" want, over the years community colleges have retained a steadfast commitment to try to respond.
When the people questioned the dominance of the transfer function, for
example, community colleges gave them vocational dominance, revers-
ing the balance from one-third vocational to two-thirds vocational in little more than a decade. That's "too vocational," said the people. When
the people asked for access to all, regardless of past achievement, the
open door swung wide to admit, to many colleges, a majority of students

B. L. Johnson, (Ed.). *New Directions for Community Colleges: General Education in Two-Year Colleges,* no. 40.
San Francisco: Jossey-Bass, December 1982.

unable to perform at the college level. There are "no standards," said the people. It is hard to know whether the people's colleges should be responsive to the times or stand firm for enduring values.

General education shares some of these problems of the community colleges. General education is the people's education, responsive to the changing needs of students and society—or, wait, is it the people's ideal, true to enduring values across the ages? General education, it is said, is rooted in the universals of human culture (Hutchins, 1967); it is preparation for participation in a democratic society (President's Commission on Higher Education, 1948); it is a corrective to the overemphasis of specialization (Meiklejohn, 1920); it is the common knowledge and common values on which a free society depends (Harvard Committee, 1945).

Diversity in General Education — A Constant

Diversity in both interpretation and implementation of general education is not only permissible but has been seen as desirable over the years. As Johnson wrote in 1952, "One of the most heartening features about this report is the great diversity of content and methods in the general education programs of the California junior colleges. This is a healthy condition, for it indicates that institutions believe in adapting their offerings to the needs of their own students" (p. xix). In 1981 that thesis was repeated by the twelve-college General Education Models (GEM) Consortium, which deliberately sought diversity in their membership because "we wanted to discourage schools from merely adopting some variation of the 'Harvard Plan' that was getting much publicity at the time. The best way to encourage creative thinking, we reasoned, was to include a wide range of different kinds of schools and to urge each to develop a program tailored to its own needs and circumstances" (Wee, 1981, p. 5).

The premise that general education programs may be diverse and may appear in many forms seems to be one of the universals of general education over the years.

Certainly, the goal of today's reformers of general education is not to promote a singular new or improved model of general education, as was the case in certain reforms of the past such as the "great books" (Meiklejohn, 1920) or the Harvard Redbook (Harvard Committee, 1945), but to gain heightened recognition for and action toward the ideal of integration, coherence, and shared values and concerns in the college curriculum.

Waves of Reform in General Education

Reform movements for general education seem to appear about every thirty years, some think in response to cyclic tensions in the society that threaten disintegration and isolation. Boyer and Levine (1980) identify three periods of general education reform in this century and note that each seemed to have its origins in the disintegration of community in the broader society. The first reform movement occurred in the 1920s, starting with Alexander Meiklejohn's introduction of the survey course at Amherst and reaching its height in Robert Hutchins's required curriculum in the "great books" at the University of Chicago in 1928.

The second wide-scale revival of general education came on the heels of World War II. In 1945, the Harvard Committee's report, *General Education in a Free Society,* dubbed the "Redbook," became the bible for reform on campuses nationwide, despite the fact that the Harvard faculty rejected most of its proposals. In 1948, the President's Commission on Higher Education called for reform, stating: "The crucial task of higher education today... is to provide a unified general education for American youth. Colleges must find the right relationship between specialized training on the one hand, aiming at a thousand different careers, and the transmission of a common cultural heritage toward a common citizenship on the other" (p. 49).

It was in this climate that the California Study of General Education in the Junior College was launched with a six-week general education workshop in the summer of 1951. Although by today's standards a study of general education limited to the community colleges of California would be considered parochial, in 1951 over half of the junior college students of the nation were enrolled in the public junior colleges of California.

Today we are caught up in the third big wave of reform, cropping up in many places but sparked by the Carnegie Foundation studies of the college curriculum (Boyer and Levine, 1980; Carnegie Foundation, 1977, 1981; Levine, 1978; Rudolph, 1977), by Harvard's well-publicized "core curriculum" (1979), and, in the community colleges, by Miami–Dade's three-year reform of general education (Lukenbill and McCabe, 1978).

Most reforms start with generally uncomplimentary observations about the existing situation. The 1952 study of general education in the junior colleges of California was undertaken because the "present confusion about the character of general education must be resolved" (Johnson, 1952, p. viii). Recently the oft-quoted words of the Carnegie Foundation that general education is a "disaster area" (1977) ring in the ears. Less frequently quoted is the next sentence, which claims that general education "has been on the defensive and losing ground for more than 100 years" (p. 11) — which doesn't say very much for the lasting impact of the two earlier reform movements in this century.

In fact, over the years, general education seems to have been a kind of special target for community college analysts. In 1960, Medsker wrote, "The data. . .lead inescapably to the conclusion that junior colleges have made relatively little progress in developing well-organized curricula for general education" (p. 63). Thorton (1966) sounded the criticism again in the mid-1960s: "The evidence is conclusive that public junior colleges have not yet, in practice, accepted general education as one of their primary purposes" (p. 209). And, in 1982, Cohen and Brawer observed that "general education has remained a noble idea but a practical backwater in most American higher education" (p. 316).

Current Status of General Education

My assignment is to try to determine what has happened in the thirty years that have passed since the first major study of general education in the community colleges. It seems clear that general education has always been an avowed mission of community colleges. It seems equally clear that it has never been a primary mission. Often squeezed from sight and mind by the bigger and stronger forces of transfer and vocational education, which are in constant tension for supremacy, general education could be the common ground on which to establish cooperation. But in thirty years of spectacular growth and momentum in community colleges, the relative position of general education has changed little. General education in the community college is neither more secure nor less than it was thirty years ago, neither more clarified nor more blurred, neither more important nor less. From time to time it sparks real fervor, exciting innovation, and the rededication of students and faculty to the enduring values of education. Upon occasion, general education has shown itself to be so basic to the overall purposes of education that a faculty starting out to evaluate the general education requirements ends by restructuring and rethinking the purposes and practices of their entire institution.

Such has been the case at Miami–Dade Community College (see Chapter Nine). A project that was launched in 1975 to study the inevitable complaints that general education at the college lacked integration and coherence turned into massive institutional reform that is having an impact on the purposes, philosophy, and practices throughout that institution and far beyond. But, historically, community colleges have shown little interest in innovation related to general education. Harrison (1973) claims that "the community college has been unable to move in any significant way toward an implementation of general education that is unique to the community college movement" (p. 91). And the intensive efforts of a recent team of investigators to locate innovative community college general education programs turned up only two — Los Medanos in California and Miami–Dade (Hammons, Thomas, and Ward, 1980).

One small question lies at the heart of general education reform: What should every college student know? The question may be small, but it is not simple. What a student needs to know does not usually refer narrowly to content but may include generalized insights, specific skills, broad understandings, and sometimes even motivation. Wick (1981), for example, says that "general education should not focus on *what* is learned, but rather on *how* to learn" (p. 8), and the Miami–Dade rationale asserts that "general education can stimulate students to develop a positive attitude toward further learning to meet their personal and career needs throughout life" (Lukenbill and McCabe, 1978, p. 31).

When this question is taken seriously, there is no turning back from a variety of troubling questions about how the college will assure itself that all students have learned what all students need to know. How do students who are grossly deficient in reading and writing learn what they need to know to survive in the information society? How can teachers be held accountable in classrooms in which student diversity is so great that there is no way to define, let alone teach, the "average" student? If the faculty members really believe that there are certain skills, understandings, and knowledge that every student should have, when has the college met its obligation — when the curriculum is available? when the requirements are established? when 70 percent of the students meet the requirements?

Answers to these questions may be more far-reaching and lead to deeper and more permanent changes than merely the dutiful revision of the general education curriculum. The trouble is that not many people take these questions seriously, and general education is more likely to lead to conflicts over "turf," politics, and abstractions than over the realities of mass education. It is fairly easy to trace the fortunes and misfortunes of general education as a concept over the decades; it is far more difficult to evaluate its impact on education and society.

In the thirty years since the appearance of *General Education in Action* (Johnson, 1952), there have been some constants in general education, some specifics that speak to the climate of the times, and always diversity in interpretation and implementation. Even the "constants" change in emphasis and priority, however. For example, it would be difficult to imagine a list of general educational goals that failed to mention the need for students to be competent in the basic skills — usually meaning reading, writing, and arithmetic, but sometimes embellished with less commonly stated skills such as listening, foreign languages, aesthetics, and so forth. Despite constant and universal agreement that the basic skills are part of general education, the attitudes toward them vary considerably. Right now, for example, there is near panic over the failure of community college students — or four-year college students, for that matter — to demonstrate mastery of (and sometimes even familiarity with) the three R's. So today one is likely to find discussions of basic skills stripped to the essentials and combined with requirements and standards for graduation (Lukenbill and McCabe, 1978).

If aspirations for complex cognitive development seem to be less ambitious in 1982 than in 1952, the aspirations for personal development have taken a turn toward greater sophistication and complexity. "Know thyself" is another "constant" in general education that appears in every age, but with changing emphases and interpretations. In 1952, for example, Johnson considered the guidance program sufficiently integral to general education programs in community colleges to devote a full chapter to it, claiming that "the guidance program becomes of central importance to the junior college, its administration and faculty, to its program of general education, and to its students" (p. 55).

In 1982, two profound changes have taken place in the way we think about personal development. First and foremost, the lifelong learning movement has introduced a new lexicon (such as "adult stages of development" and "life cycles"), and Gail Sheehy's best-selling book, *Passages: Predictable Crises of Adult Life* (1976), has made everyone (but especially the adult-populated community colleges) aware that personal development is a lifelong process and that each phase of life has its unique challenges and characteristics.

A second change that has occurred in the interpretation of the general education goal of self-understanding is related to the first in its emphasis on self-direction as an adult reponsibility. In 1952, a primary responsibility of student personnel services was to collect information about students and to use such information in accordance with "professional judgment." But thirty years have passed (or maybe only twenty) since it was considered appropriate to send instructors "selected and carefully interpreted data" or to make information about students available to them "when appropriate," as recommended in the California study (Johnson, 1952, p. 71).

These changes have the general effect of moving self-under-standing and personal development out of the extracurricular realm into the curriculum itself. Today, most (52 percent) community college educators do *not* consider the guidance program part of their general education program (Hammons, Thomas, and Ward, 1980), and Cohen and Brawer (1982) are unsympathetic to broadening the definition of general education to include any experience beyond what we ordinarily think of as courses — structured, organized sequences of the curriculum. In other words, instead of counselors "interpreting" the problems of a student in ways consistent with professional understanding of the stages of adult development and then advising the student accordingly, counselors today are more likely to be teaching a class on personal development. Thus many community colleges now require some type of course on personal development as part of a basic core curriculum (Lukenbill and McCabe, 1978; Sweeney, 1981). Others provide experiences in self-direction; Los Medanos College, for example, requires self-directed study as part of the general education package. "A person learns to be autonomous (self-directive and self-responsible) by having experiences in autonomy" (Collins, 1978, p. 12).

Other changes in general education between 1952 and 1982 are more subtle. One of the enduring constants of general education is the battle against specialization and fractionalization. The Carnegie Foundation's (Boyer, 1981) emphasis on "those experiences, relationships, and ethical concerns that are common to all of us simply by virtue of our membership in the human family" (p. 8) and in Maryland, Catonsville Community College's design of interdisciplinary core courses echo Mark Van Doren's (1943) observations on "the connectedness of things" and Woodrow Wilson's call for a general education program at Princeton that would focus on experience and thoughts that were common to students. Integration, common knowledge, and shared experiences have been recurring themes of general education over the years. There is, however, a subtle difference in emphasis between "getting it together" within the individual and "getting it together" as a society. General education in the 1980s seems to take a broader sweep, focusing less on the individual and more on the "connectedness" of things and people than did the 1950s' general education.

This broader approach is especially apparent in the six themes recently proposed by the Carnegie Foundation for the Advancement of Teaching (Boyer, 1981). Those themes are (1) students should come to understand the shared use of symbols; (2) students should understand their shared membership in groups and institutions; (3) students should

understand that everyone produces and consumes and that, through this process, we are dependent on each other; (4) all life forms on the planet earth are inextricably interlocked, and no education is complete without an understanding of the ordered, interdependent nature of the universe; (5) all students should understand our shared sense of time; (6) all students should explore our shared values and beliefs.

Of the six goals for general education at Miami–Dade (Lukenbill and McCabe, 1978), the first three—competence in the fundamental skills, self-understanding, and future planning—are directed toward learning for individual enhancement, but the remaining three stress relationships with other persons, with society, and with the natural environment. While the 1952 goals for general education did not ignore interdependencies, there appeared to be more confidence that if "good individuals" could be developed, interrelationships would take care of themselves. "Life-adjustment education" was a nationwide program designed to help individuals fit comfortably into the society in which they found themselves. Proponents of general education in the 1950s talked frequently about common needs and common responsibilities, but they were less likely to talk about shared concerns.

Finally, the functionalism that seemed to be the recommended direction for community college general education in the 1950s is not so clear now. Functionalism attempts to organize education around "problem areas" or functions instead of in terms of traditional subject matter fields. It is student-centered, having its roots in the progressive belief that methods of critical thought are lifelong skills, while bodies of knowledge are continually changing. As reasonable as that sounds, especially in community colleges where student-centered education has generally enjoyed more support than in more traditional institutions, there is not much evidence that the organization of the general education curriculum into problem areas is the direction of the future. Participants in the GEM Consortium, which consisted of an unusually diverse set of institutions including some community colleges, found themselves agreeing to some extent with each of the four philosophies of general education defined by Arthur Levine (1978): (1) Perennialism focuses on the development of rational faculties through common educational substance for everyone; it is often expressed through the "great books" approach to general education. (2) Essentialism is a teacher-centered view that stresses an "essential" body of knowledge to transmit the cultural heritage of humankind. (3) Progressivism is comparable to functionalism as it was used in the 1952 report, leading to a student-centered, problem-oriented curriculum. (4) Reconstructionism emphasizes the restructuring of society. It is hard to find any "pure" forms of these philosophies in the general educational programs of the 1980s; the direction seems to be mostly toward eclecticism.

The Future of General Education

Where to now with general education? It is hard to say. Today's authorities differ. Levine (1981) is convinced that "general education reform has a great deal going for it today — timing, student interest, and enhanced faculty support" (p. 137). He finds the 1980s a "uniquely propitious" time for strengthening general education. Gaff (1980) says only that today's tremendous activity "virtually guarantees that general education will be different in the future than it is today" (p. 5).

I believe that most of the current reform movements in general education fail to comprehend fully the revolutionary impact of adult part-time learners on the college curriculum. It is too early to predict the shape of that revolution, but it involves technology, the measurement of education in terms of competencies rather than courses, and the consideration of providers of education for adults other than traditional colleges and universities. Even in the face of the enormous impact on the shape of education that any one of these changes suggests, it is a reasonably safe bet that the reform of general education will be on the agenda again soon after the turn of the century.

References

Boyer, E. "The Quest for Common Learning: A Carnegie Colloquium on General Education." In The Carnegie Foundation for the Advancement of Teaching, *Common Learning.* Washington, D.C.: The Carnegie Foundation for the Advancement of Teaching, 1981.

Boyer, E., and Levine, A. *A Quest for Common Learning.* Washington, D.C.: The Carnegie Foundation for the Advancement of Teaching, 1980.

The Carnegie Foundation for the Advancement of Teaching. *Missions of the College Curriculum.* San Francisco: Jossey-Bass, 1977.

The Carnegie Foundation for the Advancement of Teaching. *Common Learning: A Carnegie Colloquium on General Education.* Washington, D.C.: The Carnegie Foundation for the Advancement of Teaching, 1981.

Cohen, A. M., and Brawer, F. *The American Community College.* San Francisco: Jossey-Bass, 1982.

Collins, C. C. "General Education at Los Medanos College: A Curricular Model." Paper presented at the Danforth Foundation Conference on General and Liberal Education, St. Louis, March 16–18, 1978.

Gaff, J. G. "General Education for a Contemporary Context." In *Current Issues in Higher Education: New Models for General Education.* Washington, D.C.: American Association for Higher Education, 1980.

Hammons, J., Thomas, W., and Ward, S. "General Education in the Community College." *Community College Frontiers,* Spring 1980, pp. 22–28.

20

Harrison, J. D. "General Education in the Community College: A Recent Review." *Journal of General Education,* July 1973, pp. 83–93.

Harvard Committee. *General Education in a Free Society.* Cambridge, Mass.: Harvard University Press, 1945.

Harvard University. "Report on the Core Curriculum." Cambridge, Mass.: Faculty of Arts and Sciences, 1979.

Hutchins, R. M. *The Higher Learning in America.* New Haven, Conn.: Yale University Press, 1967.

Johnson, B. L. *General Education in Action.* Washington, D.C.: American Council on Education, 1952.

Levine, A. "Prospects for the Future." In Carnegie Foundation for the Advancement of Teaching, *Common Learning: A Carnegie Colloquium on General Education.* Washington, D.C.: Carnegie Foundation for the Advancement of Teaching, 1981.

Levine, A. *Handbook on Undergraduate Education.* San Francisco: Jossey-Bass, 1978.

Lukenbill, J. D., and McCabe, R. H. *General Education in a Changing Society.* Dubuque, Iowa: Kendall/Hunt, 1978.

Medsker, L. L. *The Junior College: Progress and Prospect.* New York: McGraw-Hill, 1960.

Meiklejohn, A. *The Liberal College.* Boston: Marshall Jones, 1920.

President's Commission on Higher Education. *Higher Education for American Democracy.* New York: Harper, 1948.

Rudolph, F. *Curriculum: A History of the American Undergraduate Course of Study Since 1636.* San Francisco: Jossey-Bass, 1977.

Sheehy, G. *Passages: Predictable Crises of Adult Life.* New York: Dutton, 1976.

Sweeney, R. "A Description of General Education at the Community College of Denver." *GEM Newsletter,* August 1981, pp. 1–4.

Thorton, J. W. *The Community College.* New York: Wiley, 1966.

Van Doren, M. *Liberal Education.* New York: Henry Holt, 1943.

Wee, D. *On General Education: Guidelines for Reform.* New Haven, Conn.: Society for Values in Higher Education, 1981.

Wick, D. L. "In Defense of Knowledge: An Intellectual Framework for General Education." *Change,* September 1981, pp. 8–9.

K. Patricia Cross is visiting professor, Graduate School of Education, Harvard University.

"Since all education today is, and must be, both liberal and vocational, the task is not that of finding the appropriate proportions of each but rather of reappraising and redefining all courses so that they contribute to both"
(Dressel, 1959, p. 4).

General Education and Vocational Education

Melvin L. Barlow

For the most part the relationship between general education and vocational education has been not a controversial issue but rather a misunderstood one. Few people in the area of general education have ever had a total view of the background, goals, and purposes of vocational education, and the converse is equally true. The idea that anyone could separate general education and vocational education into two distinct and unrelated areas is now, and always has been, false. Almost any area of education can be called general or vocational depending upon the intent of the student. For persons who intend to earn their living as historians, the study of history is as vocational as is the study of automotive technology for persons who intend to earn their living as automotive technologists. In many respects, these two areas of education are, and should be, miscible — that is, like certain liquids, each dissolves into the other.

In this chapter, we analyze several major aspects of the relationship between general education and vocational education and suggest ways in which the general goals of education can emerge in and through vocational education.

B. L. Johnson, (Ed.). *New Directions for Community Colleges: General Education in Two-Year Colleges,* no. 40.
San Francisco: Jossey-Bass, December 1982.

The Rise of Vocational Education

Vocational education developed during the early years of the twentieth century with the specific intent of preparing people for the world of work. This focus, however, did not mean the divorce of vocational education from the other areas of education.

When free public education ideas first were receiving general acceptance after 1820, many references indicated a need for the inclusion of a new subject matter area. The schools of the Manual Labor Movement in the 1830s and 1840s, a variety of special schools around the time of the Civil War, the lyceums and mechanics institutes, and the private trade schools were all examples of the growing need to enlarge the educational sphere. But the transformation was not easy — it was somewhat like throwing a bucket of water upwind. Mays (1946) summarized this early period as a time when the educator regarded the school as a place of books and abstract knowledge; anything else was tyranny.

During the early years of the twentieth century, however, the pressures from economic forces outside the schools called for specific vocational education, and these forces were too great to be ignored. Scores of prominent educators discussed the problem, and it appeared that the alleged conflict between the vocational and the general education was pretty much one of interpretation rather than fact.

After years of study, and because vocational education was considered to be a national issue, Congress possed the Smith-Hughes Act in 1917. Congress had previously passed the Land Grant College Act in 1862, but the 1917 act was directed toward the secondary schools of the nation. Only seventy-six junior colleges had been established by 1917 (sixteen of these were in California), and their potential contribution to the vocational education needs of youth and adults was less than nil. At that time, it would have been sheer folly to plan and develop the vocational education program around the junior college.

It was clearly stated in the Smith-Hughes Act that "the controlling purpose of such education shall be to fit students for useful employment." It was also clear that half of the school day was to be devoted to other subjects offered in the secondary school. Joining the general and the vocational areas was thus mandated in the federal regulations for vocational education; the predominant feeling, then, was that these essential areas of education were not to be separate for the full-time student.

By 1920, vocational education had become firmly established as a public school function, although some educators were alarmed that it engendered too great an enthusiasm. The National Education Association, for example, "would stress the crying need that the general or cultural education must not be overshadowed by vocational training" (Mays, 1946, p. 82). The Commission on the Reorganization of Secondary Education included education for vocation as one of its cardinal principles but stressed the relationship of citizenship and vocational education: "This commission... stands squarely for the infusion of vocation with the spirit of service and for the vitalization of culture by genuine contact with the world's work" (Owen, 1921, p. 165).

The idea that citizenship could be enhanced in and through vocational education was also expressed by Senator Carroll S. Page during his speech before the Senate on July 24, 1916, when he said: "I submit, Mr. President, that this can be done [achieve good citizenship] in no way so well as by vocational education—indeed it is probable that there is no other way in which it can be done at all" (Page, 1916).

The fact is that the literature of vocational education contains many references indicating that general education and vocational education were not to be thought of as separate entities. But differences of opinion persisted. The root cause of these differences may have been just plain ignorance about the goals of both these areas of education.

Liberal Education and Vocational Training

Perhaps one of the most significant and cogent statements ever made concerning the relationship of general education and vocational education was provided by philosophy professor Theodore M. Greene (1955) of Yale. It is reproduced in part here as the keynote of our definition of this relationship:

"Liberal education" and "vocational training" should be conceived of neither as hostile rivals nor as mutually exclusive enterprises but, on the contrary, as two essential and complementary aspects of the total preparation of the individual for his total life... It is an everlasting pity that so sharp a dichotomy has established itself in our minds between liberal education and vocational training, with the false implication that the former is somehow higher, though useless, and the latter, useful but somehow crass and demeaning. If these two equally essential preparations for life are thus divorced, a *merely* liberal education will indeed tend to be useless, and a *merely* vocational training, crass. What is obviously needed is a truly liberal academic community in which the study of art and typewriting, of philosophy and accounting, of theology and medicine, of pure and applied science are, though admittedly very different, judged to be equally honorable and valuable in their several ways [pp. 118–119].

Areas of Concern

One of the great leaders in vocational education, Franklin J. Keller (1948), spent much of his life putting into educational practice his hallmark, "the primacy of the person." Education existed for the benefit of students, claimed Keller, not as a convenience for instructors, administrators, boards of trustees, and the general development of institutions. Keller sought what was best for students, not just what was best for the institution, the instructors, or the administration. Yet one of the prime problems in establishing the relationship between general and vocational education has been that vocational education does not fit into the regular school mold.

The Full-Time Student. Many of the community colleges develop integrated programs of general education and vocational education that lead to an associate degree or an appropriate certificate. Students of these programs have a double benefit: They are not only prepared to launch a useful and productive working career but they are also able to emphasize other aspects of education that will enhance their careers.

On the other hand, some students enter community college programs of vocational education for the sole purpose of preparing for a job, and they elect only courses that are related directly to such preparation. Some ignore the potential for developing competencies in other areas. It is possible that these students did not seek counseling assistance, or it was not available to them, and that they were not aware of the availability of other related pursuits. But the point is that full-time community college students in vocational education are in an excellent position to sample areas of education that emphasize general values and in turn, to recognize these values in their vocational courses.

The Part-Time Student. A majority of vocational education enrollments in community colleges are represented by students who are working and who desire only such courses that upgrade and update their occupational skills or that provide opportunities for advanced training in their present occupations. In many cases, these students, who may be working either full-time or part-time, are seeking retraining for a new job. Part-time students also include some persons who are entering employment for the first time. Surprisingly, a number of these students have already completed a baccalaureate degree in an area that did not prepare them for the labor market.

Of the nearly 10,000 students at the West Valley Occupational Center (conducted by the Los Angeles City Schools), 36 percent of the students are high school graduates, 30.6 percent have completed one to three years of college, and 11.4 percent have completed four or more years of college. This successful educational venture, which places 85 percent of its students in jobs, is made possible in part by excellent cooperation with the world of work.

Similar statistics for part-time students are also to be found in community colleges, but what may be lacking in such programs are cooperation efforts within the institutions between the general and the vocational areas. If general education concepts are interwoven logically with vocational pursuits, then vocational education can have a wide-ranging impact on part-time students. There are some limitations, however, the most significant of which are time and the extreme variations in the quality of these students' educational backgrounds. Still, some of the general educational goals inherent in vocational instruction are achieved almost automatically, such as standards of work, pride in workmanship, relationships among workers, responsibility, interdependence of workers, management of human and material resources, honesty, and a host of other desirable social, personal, and civic concerns.

Cooperation. One thing that is needed to improve the overall quality of education is greater cooperation, concern, and sensitivity from both the general and vocational groups. Few people in the general education area pay much attention to vocational education, and few people in vocational education pay much attention to general education. The availability of one group to the other is very important.

The college catalogue, for example, which titles courses as vocational or as general, tends to create a problem that cries out for a solution. The idea that certain general goals of education can be pursued only in certain courses is false. Listing subjects under such headings as "general education" or "vocational education" forces a dichotomy where none exists. The qualities or characteristics that have to do with "vocationalness" or "generalness" simply do not depend upon the name of the subject. It is the *intent of the individual* that makes a subject become vocational or general — *not the name of the subject.* It is the practice in vocational education to place students who have common vocational interests in one class. This practice facilitates administration and instruction, but it is not the name of the subject that makes it vocational.

General education focuses attention upon goals that are desirable for all persons; admittedly, certain subject matter areas contribute more toward some of these goals than others, but it was never intended that general education consist of a defined list of subject matter areas. The subject matter of vocational education can make real contributions toward achieving some of the goals of general education. Unfortunately, neither the vocationalists nor the generalists have shown much interest in the cooperation that will make these contributions possible.

California's Statewide Longitudinal Study

The statewide longitudinal study (Hunter and Sheldon, 1980) of students in fifteen of California's community colleges brought to light a number of issues related to vocational education. The researchers classified the students in vocational education into five categories: (1) vocational career program completer; (2) job seeker; (3) student interested in improving job skills; (4) second careerist; and (5) the license maintainer. In comparing the vocational education student and the nonvocational (general education) student, Hunter and Sheldon (1980) reported:

> Comparisons between vocational and nonvocational students provided no important differences in demographics. Little difference was observed in grade point average, but vocational students were more productive in credit earned than nonvocational students. In addition, vocational students completed objectives more completely, had fewer conflicts with their jobs, and had a better understanding of their college goals than nonvocational students. They also had higher skill-level jobs and were more highly paid than nonvocational students [p. 61].

The Intrinsic Perspective

The intrinic values of vocational education frequently escape the attention of educators as these vales are not as obvious as the extrinsic values. Silberman (1979) reports that "in the intrinsic perspective, income and future placement are secondary concerns, and human development and personal satisfaction with the experiences provided in the program are primary" (p. 48).

Although Silberman's article focuses attention on the high school, his points of view are equally meaningful at the community college level. He describes five dimensions in which a well-designed vocational education program can promote human development: "First, vocational projects can provide an area in which students obtain a sense of personal competence. A second dimension for personal growth is aesthetic expression. A third dimension for personal growth is integrity. A fourth dimension for personal growth is cooperativeness. A fifth dimension of personal growth is a heightened sense of altruism" (p. 49).

These dimensions are not foreign to the principles upon which vocational education was developed more than seventy-five years ago. The system was visualized as one in which education and preparation for work were integrated. Skills, knowledge, attitudes, and appreciations were key goals for each vocational education program but were not limited entirely to the role of job preparation. A person's cultural heritage was extremely important. As Silberman suggests, a basis for such personal development exists in vocational education programs.

Vocational Education — General Education's Last Opportunity

It would be impossible to remove the *general* aspects from vocational education, even if one wanted to do so. For some students, vocational education represents the last chance the school may have to impart some of the general goals that are considered imperative for all students. To date, we have not even scratched the surface of the opportunity that vocational education offers for students to achieve the general goals of education. Great imagination and commitment among institutions, administrators, and instructors are necessary to promote these goals. (Simply forcing a student to repeat a course in which he failed doesn't do the job.)

Take the case of the community college that devised a vast array of scientific experiments as an integral part of the vocational education program. Students in welding, dressmaking, electronics, and all other vocational programs conducted experiments directly related to their area of learning, and these experiments initiated further interest among the students. Some students took other science and related courses. A group of cosmetology teachers became enthusiastic about the program and encouraged a community college chemistry instructor to offer a special course in the chemistry of cosmetology. This program was conducted as a university extension course and was offered for many years.

A carpentry instructor in one college built a house as a class project that ran throughout the year. The project became an all-school activity with many departments involved and even included representatives from the community in the basic architecture, stress analysis, and color design for the building. The entire community was well aware of the project, and the house was sold by the school board at the end of the year. The project was repeated during the following years.

An instructor of cabinet making conducted his vocation education program as a regular business and involved other departments in the school. Each student's project had to be cost-effective; thus, the business phase of the program was conducted by the business department. The English department assisted in report writing and many other related activities. The close cooperation among the various departments of the school and the vocational education program provided additional meaning for the students.

An instructor in petroleum technology utilized the community resources so that the educational program was closely related to the real-life employment situation. In addition, the departments of English, science, and engineering were closely related to the program, and instructors from history, psychology, chemistry, and mathematics participated generously.

Many examples exist where close relationships have been established between the vocational and the general education areas. Such relationships do not happen automatically; they must be planned, and they depend on cooperation among faculty members and on an administration willing to try out new ideas for the benefit of the students.

The Action Line — A Summary

At first glance, the theme of this chapter appears to be about general education within the framework of vocational education. But the theme runs much deeper: it concerns people — all kinds of people, but with an emphasis on people in community colleges. The theme, therefore, is larger than mere discussions about the relative merits of educational areas but becomes a theme about how these areas can help people.

There are countless opportunities to make the general goals of education an active part of vocational instruction. We know that this does happen — sometimes by accident but also on purpose. The point is that it does not happen on purpose as frequently as it could. Someone has to take the first step in order to improve this situation. This first step is probably the responsibility of the administration of a community college. Experienced general and vocational educators working cooperatively — in the interests of people, not subjects — can find the ways and means of achieving the general goals of education in vocational areas. There are no formulas to follow; the success of action plans depends entirely upon the creative genius of the faculty of an institution.

References

Dressel, P. "Liberal and Vocational Education." *College and University Bulletin*. Washington, D.C.: Association for Higher Education, 1959.

Greene, T. M. "A Liberal Christian Idealist's Philosophy of Education." In N. B. Henry (Ed.), *Modern Philosophies and Education: The Fifty-Fourth Yearbook of the National Society for the Study of Education, Part I*. Chicago: University of Chicago Press, 1955.

Hunter, R., and Sheldon, M. S. *Statewide Longitudinal Study: Report on Academic Year 1979–80, Part III, Fall Results*. Los Angeles: Los Angeles Pierce College, 1980.

Keller, F. J. "Primacy of the Person." *Principles of Vocational Education*. New York: D. C. Heath, 1948.

Mays, A. B. "The Concept of Vocational Education in the Thinking of the General Educator, 1845 to 1945." *University of Illinois Bulletin,* 1946, *43* (65).

Owen, W. B. *The Report of the Commission on the Reorganization of Secondary Education*. Washington, D.C.: National Education Association, 1921.

Page, C. S. *Congressional Record,* July 24, 1916, pp. 13264–13265.

Silberman, H. F. "High School Vocational Education: An Intrinsic Perspective." *UCLA Educator,* 1979, *21* (1).

Melvin L. Barlow is professor of vocational education, emeritus, University of California, Los Angeles.

They can learn! They simply have not been
taught to read, to write, to figure.

Literacy Development: Foundation for General Education

Suanne D. Roueche
John E. Roueche

No matter whose definition for general education one uses, a basic underlying requirement is that enrolling college students will be able to read, write, study, and figure well enough to be successful in freshman courses.

That entering students in American community colleges are severely deficient in the skills of basic literacy has been well documented by both popular and scholarly writers over the past decade. These human shortcomings pose serious problems for the very survival of our society. Astin's latest study (1982) documents rampant grade inflation in public schools as the major contributing factor to the continued decline in the academic abilities of today's college students. An astonishing 60 percent of the students agreed that grading standards in high schools are much too easy.

If general education is to prepare our learners for effective living in contemporary society, we have more cause for alarm. Quoting from United States Army studies, Anderson (1982) revealed that "almost 40

B. L. Johnson, (Ed.). *New Directions for Community Colleges: General Education in Two-Year Colleges*, no. 40.
San Francisco: Jossey-Bass, December 1982.

percent of the Army's junior enlisted personnel read below the 5.5 grade level, which is 'functionally illiterate' by United Nations standards. A startling 23 percent can't read as well as kids in the third grade. One soldier in fifty doesn't have sufficient grasp of English to understand orders. More than half can't comprehend manuals that already have been rewritten to the seventh grade level" (pp. 16–17).

American community colleges are reporting today that more than half of the entering freshman class reads below the eighth grade level even though they have graduated from high school. A California president of an urban community college has reported that 92 percent of last fall's freshmen scored below the eighth grade level on the college required Nelson-Denny Reading Test. These statistics also help to explain why most open-access colleges are losing, through failure and attrition, upwards of 50 percent of each fall's entering group of students.

Finally, colleges are discovering that basic literacy is more of an essential prerequisite today than at any time in human history. For example, a number of community colleges have lately assessed the readability levels of textbooks, laboratory manuals, technical and career manuals, and various specification manuals used in freshman courses. The results are astonishing! No more than one community college course in fifty has language requirements below the twelfth grade reading level. And perhaps most surprising of all, the most verbally demanding of all programs today in American community colleges are to be found in career areas.

The Community College Response

Community colleges have reluctantly (yet forcefully) faced up to the realities of enrolling students who are barely literate in super sophisticated literacy-demanding college courses. Discussing the "skills for living," as defined by the Dallas County Community College Taskforce for Common Learning, Shaw and Alfers (1982) summarized the dilemma well:

> In earlier times, the "basics" (reading, writing, and arithmetic) were not considered a part of general education. Rather, they were fundamental to it. Today, one cannot assume that all students are competent in these areas. The Dallas County Community College District adheres to the belief that these skills are basic to effective living, and is committed to producing graduates who are competent in reading, writing, and computation. The development of these skills is a priority throughout the district and is fundamental to the general education provided by "Skills for Living" [p. 1].

To attack the problem institutionally and directly, Dawson College in Montreal established a Senate Literacy Committee (1981) that recommended the following:

1. The college, each sector and each department, should endorse the principle that literacy is the responsibility of *every* teacher and *every* department of the college.

2. Each department should formulate means by which its teachers can help improve students' literacy, such as:

a. Increasing the number of short written assignments throughout the term

b. Giving more short, structured reading assignments

c. Teaching students how to read the course materials, and producing a pamphlet or handbook that specifies correct form and style for written work in that course or department

d. Asking students to rewrite unclear or careless work after the teacher has corrected at least some of the errors in English and has explained why the work is unacceptable

e. Stressing the indissolubility of clear thought with its expression in words or numbers; stressing to students that form and content are one; marking for both form and content.

3. The college, as a whole, should recognize that all English core courses teach students *how* to read books and *how* to write papers as well as teach the literature of our common culture.

The Provincial Literacy Committee in Quebec made similar recommendations to all colleges across the province (Senate Literacy Committee, 1981). Specific ones include:

1. Colleges must assume a general responsibility for the development of English language skills among their students.

2. All teachers must actively encourage students in their courses to value effective use of language. Specific suggestions here include the assignment of more term papers, written exams, and as many short essays as possible; faculty-written commentary on language use in all written work; grades based on form as well as content across the curriculum; and that all departments must make students increasingly aware that effective use of language is a valuable academic, professional, and personal asset.

A key point to be made here is that skill-deficient students are not lacking in cognitive ability or in aptitude for learning. Today's students simply have not been taught to read, write, or figure. But they can learn!

The University of Texas Study

After an intensive three-year investigation of literacy demands across community college courses, we concluded that for systematic development to occur in the community college, there must be organized and concerted administrative and instructional effort to effect it. The following points summarize other important conclusions drawn from the University of Texas study (Roueche and Comstock, 1981):

1. There is a separation between the administrative organization of departments and programs and the academic careers of students. Different departments and programs of the college possess such a high degree of autonomy in curriculum design that it often results in overlaps among courses with similar goals.

2. Some courses that have traditionally been required of all degree-seeking students and that are intended to serve students in both academic and vocational programs have weak links between themselves and the programs they purport to serve.

3. "Skill" courses, usually primarily concerned with teaching the basic skills of reading, writing, and math, serve general functions but are likely to be integrated only loosely with the other courses to which they can be directly linked (for example, reading and writing with English).

4. Faculty assumptions about the nature of basic skills are heavily influenced by their training and by the textbooks they use: They generally conceive of skills as being independent of context; in other words, there is little or no attempt to link learning activities to the types of tasks or problem situations that the students would be likely to encounter in other classrooms or in the practice of a vocation.

5. The less relevant course content appears to the student and the more pressured he or she is for time, the more likely that the student will merely attempt to find out what the instructor wants and give only that much effort. The more relevant the course content appears, the more inclined the student is to try to get more from a course than just a passing grade.

6. Types of knowledge transmitted by the course determine the strategies that students use to meet the literacy demands. The farther the content is removed from a familiar framework or from relevancy to other demands, the more likely the student is to resort to rote learning activities. The more familiar and relevant the content, the more likely the student is to ask questions on relationships.

7. Reading and writing are not required across the curriculum in purposeful ways; low-level cognitive activities are typical instructional and evaluative strategies.

8. Students do not read texts that are considered too difficult and that have content removed from practicality (particularly when instructors cover the same content in class); they do read texts identified as less difficult and interesting and choose to use them as "organizers" of instructors' lectures and discussions.

9. Voluntary assessment for basic skills and voluntary enrollment in developmental courses do not significantly affect the populations of those classes compared to others — that is, students enrolling in freshman English possess similar skills levels to those students who choose to enroll in the developmental sequence. Further, neither the assessment nor the development of skills appears to *predict* either student selection of courses nor performance in the college.

10. Students appear to enter the college for one of three sets of reasons: work-related goals; to work toward eventual degree-attainment; or no specific educational or occupational goals. Students who have selected a major course of study expect minimal support from counselors, and students who are undecided are more inclined to seek a counselor and educational advice. The majority of students self-advise and enter the college without orientation to college procedures, expectations, and so forth.

11. Unsuccessful experiences in college do not dampen students' enthusiasm for continuing, but they do raise questions in students' minds about the role of the institution in assessment and advisement procedures.

12. There are nonexistent or, at best, weak networks within colleges to encourage the formation of student support groups; support groups tend to consist of individuals outside the college.

13. Students have unrealistic expectations about their abilities to accommodate work and school commitments.

14. Diverse student populations bring wide differences to abilities to classrooms; instructors who attempt to provide instruction for *all* may feel compelled to make literacy demands at the lowest cognitive levels to accommodate the greatest numbers.

Concluding Recommendations

1. Organizational links between programs and the courses within programs should be instituted; full- and part-time instructors should be informed of prerequisites to the courses they teach and should be required to provide instructional links to those courses that receive

their own students; furthermore, general-function courses that are required of all degree-seeking students, as well as skill-development courses, must demonstrate that they do indeed contribute to the knowledge and skill base that students need to continue.

2. Students should not be required to negotiate material for which neither they nor the instructor can assign value and utility; there should be systematic efforts to link the content and skills learned to their purpose—that is, there should be less emphasis upon usage and more upon use.

3. Reading and writing of a purposeful nature should be required across the curriculum, rather than assigning reading and writing as disjointed activities.

4. Institutions should look to mechanisms for creating stronger student support groups within program majors and classes.

5. Assessment for basic skill development should not be voluntary; any student enrolling for any course that requires reading, writing, or figuring should be assessed for skill level. Necessary skill development should be effected *prior* to enrollment in any courses requiring it.

6. Institutions should fund developmental programs and allow students adequate *time* (and, thus, a less threatening environment) and nontraditional evaluative measures to achieve acceptable skill levels.

7. Students should be involved in active advising—whether that advising be student-initiated and then followed by counselor-initiated support or whether it be by major department representatives whose responsibilities to distinct groups of students is administered early in the student's career.

8. Improved advising for minorities and women who tend to cluster themselves in particular vocational programs should be effected to increase the likelihood that they consider the more nontraditional choices.

9. Students should not be allowed to draw course schedules that require unrealistic commitments to college; work and family commitments must be considered in light of literacy demands, and colleges should restrict attempted hours to reasonable limits.

References

Anderson, J. "Our Military's in Trouble." *Parade,* February 14, 1982, pp. 16–17.

Astin, A. "An Interview With." *U. S. News and World Report, 91* (26), January 4, 1982, pp. 87–88.

Roueche, S. D., and Comstock, V. N. *A Report on Theory and Method for the Study of Literacy Development in Community Colleges.* Technical Report NIE-400-78-0600. Austin: Program in Community College Education, The University of Texas at Austin, 1981.

Senate Literacy Committee. *Internal Memo to Faculty from Academic Dean.* Dawson College, Montreal, December 1981.

Shaw, R., and Alfers, K. *Committee Handbook for Common Learning.* Dallas: Dallas County Community College District, 1982.

Suanne D. Roueche works for the Program in Community College Education, University of Texas at Austin.

John E. Roueche is professor and director of the Program in Community College Education, University of Texas at Austin.

Citizens of all ages, backgrounds, needs, interests, and
socioeconomic circumstances are enrolling in classes —
both credit and noncredit — that are offered on campus,
at home, on the job, and at community schools,
shopping centers and libraries.

Community General Education

Ervin L. Harlacher

The community college is now pioneering the concept of community
general education. Citizens of all ages, backgrounds, needs, interests,
and socioeconomic circumstances are enrolling in classes offered on
campus, at home, on the job, and at community schools, shopping centers, and libraries; many of these courses offer no credit or promise of
economic gain. Citizens enrolled in these courses want and need personal growth as well as marketability, they want coherence and an integrated sense of knowledge as well as technical expertise, breadth as well
as depth (Chambers, 1981). They want and need perspective in their
lives.

Genesis and Definition of Community General Education

Community general education had its genesis in the community-
based education movement of the 1970s that, in turn, evolved out of the
community services and lifelong learning functions of the community
college. The focus of community-based education is on the kinds of education that community members want and need, not on what peda-
gogues think is good for them, and this education is provided where the
learners are, not where conventional college organization dictates they
should be. Lifelong learning is an umbrella "encasing everything from

B. L. Johnson, (Ed.). *New Directions for Community Colleges: General Education in Two-Year Colleges*, no. 40.
San Francisco: Jossey-Bass, December 1982.

traditional education to career training, to horizon broadening and enrichment, to coping with life" (Luskin and Chappell, 1981, p. 57).

Community general education, according to Zoglin (1979), prepares students for the responsibilities they have in common as citizens in a democracy, enables them to participate creatively in a wide range of life activities, and enhances the overall quality of life in the community. Zoglin uses the term "community general education" to "describe the body of courses designed specially to meet those needs shared by all members of the community which are not satisfied by the prebaccalaureate, occupational, or developmental curricula" (p. 29) of the community college.

The objectives of community general education are similar to those of the general education movement. Zoglin points outs that the difference lies in the fact that the community general education curriculum has been *specially designed* to meet those human needs shared by all. This is in sharp contrast to the typical general education curriculum that requires students majoring in one field to take certain courses designed for specialists in another.

A taxonomy borrowed by Reynolds (1969) from a study entitled *A Design for General Education,* published by the American Council on Education in 1944, with minor modifications, provides an accurate description of the community general education curriculum in community colleges. It includes the following subjects: health; communications; personal-social adjustment; family-marital relations; citizenship; physical environment; fine arts; personal philosophy; and recreation, including avocational pursuits.

Illustrative Programs and Practices

The increased focus of the community college on community general education is the result of three factors:
- Increased emphasis on lifelong learning
- Community-based, citizen-centered nature of the college
- Diversification of the means of responding to learner needs.

Because of these factors, the community college has discarded stereotypes long associated with other levels of education—of time, place, methodology, and people to be served.

Representative of the community college's increased emphasis on lifelong learning is the community education and services program of the Marin Community Colleges in California. Some 17,000 noncredit students enroll each quarter in a countywide program that utilizes community sites in addition to the campuses of the College of Marin and

Indian Valley Colleges. Program objectives focus on occupational and professional continuing education; community development; the family unit and the home; individual growth through counseling, cultural development, recreation, physical fitness, and basic academic/practical skills; and outreach to special populations, including older adults, handicapped, minorities, and exceptional and highly motivated children.

A second example is provided by Oklahoma City's Community Education Consortium for Lifelong Learning. The purpose of the consortium is to bring together interested community agencies and institutions, including South Oklahoma City Junior College, in order to plan ways to identify community needs and resources and to improve the quality of life in the greater Oklahoma City area.

Coastline Community College, also in California, is the prototype of the noncampus college. More than 25,000 students enroll each term in a wide array of courses offered in civic and community buildings, in commercial and professional centers, in neighborhood schools, in industrial parks, and in city parks—132 locations spread across the 105 square miles of the college district.

The Extended Learning Institute (ELI) of Northern Virginia Community College is another example of community-based education. Through an agreement between ELI and the Arlington (Virginia) County Central Library, selected ELI course materials, including audio and video tapes, textbooks, and study guides, are located at the library for use by college students and local residents. Students can obtain registration materials for each course and all the required course work at the library.

Both Coastline and Northern Virginia community colleges utilize diversified educational delivery systems in meeting community needs. Another example of diversification is provided by Kirkwood Community College in Iowa. The college utilizes both a telephone network and two-way television to connect Kirkwood's main campus and eight outlying learning centers operated by the college in the 1,000 square miles of its service area. The telephone network, Kirkwood's Talk-Listen-Confer (TLC) Telenetwork System, allows students at the eight sites near their homes to hear lectures and to take part in two-way class discussions. Moderators at the outlying sites supplement class activities through use of slides, films, and tapes. Toll-free telephone registration is available, and the college provides professional counseling on a regular basis at the centers.

In addition, the Interactive Microwave Telecommunication System at Kirkwood Community College provides two-way television interconnecting the main campus and the remote sites. Any site can be connected with any grouping of other sites. Students at these eight remote sites and at Kirkwood can see and hear each other. Additional audio and data channels interconnect these sites, allowing for computer operations at the remote sites that utilize Kirkwood's main computer on campus. In addition, four channels of instructional television fixed service (ITFS) broadcast from the main campus, covering about two-thirds of the seven-county area served by Kirkwood.

Representative community college programs from throughout the country have been selected to illustrate varied approaches to community general education in the following sections. These programs have been classified in accordance with the taxonomy suggested by Reynolds (1969): health, communications, personal-social adjustment, family-marital relations, citizenship, physical environment, fine arts, philosophy, and recreation.

Health. At Clark Technical College, twelve hours of noncredit instruction are provided to persons over sixty who desire to learn about health care maintenance in advancing years. The primary objective of the course, which emphasizes "hands on" experiences and the use of guest speakers, is to create an awareness of the skills and knowledge necessary to maintain a healthy state of being for an ill, disabled, or impaired spouse, relative, or friend. Topics include diet, medication therapy, nutrition, care for the bed patient, home safety and adaptability, specific treatments, signs of infections and illness, and first-aid techniques.

John Wood Community College in Illinois offers a unique communitywide fitness program. The two-part program features a six-week session in which students learn the physiology of exercise and nutrition's role in fitness. They are also tested for body composition and general level of fitness on the most modern equipment. In the second part of the course, students devise their own fitness program to be implemented at the community fitness agency of their choice.

Approximately 400 community residents came to the Woodbridge Campus of Northern Virginia Community College on a recent Saturday to take advantage of a health screening service. Blood tests, electrocardiograms, pap smears, oral cancer tests, blood pressure readings, and glaucoma readings were among the nineteen different health checks provided at the campus's Health Fair. Over seventy-five volunteers, including doctors, nurses, lab technicians, and members of thirteen different community organizations, participated to make the fair a success.

Communications. In 1975, Valencia Community College, Florida, and the Adult Literacy League combined resources to form the

Center for Adult Literacy at the college's open campus. The college provides general administrative and logistical support for the literacy center and the center provides training for volunteers in the Lauback method of teaching basic reading and writing to adult nonreaders. The volunteers are then assigned to work with adult nonreaders on a one-to-one basis in a place that is convenient for both of them—in churches, libraries, and community halls.

What happens when the Illinois Migrant Council, Service Employment Development (SER) Jobs for Progress, the College of Lake County and Lake County (Illinois) Comprehensive Educational Training Act (CETA) collaborate? A new comprehensive English-as-a-second-language (ESL) curriculum with a preemployment emphasis emerges. Using grammatical development as the core study area, the group developed twenty-five titles (units) ranging from personal information (writing one's own name) to banking and insurance. Using a competency-based format, the open-entrance/open-exit curriculum includes a teacher's guide, pre- and posttests, games, student work sheets, and vocabulary lists. Field testing continues with students from a wide range of national origins.

Triton College's (Illinois) Hispanic Skills Center is designed to meet the basic educational needs of the local Spanish-speaking population. Courses include English as a second language on five ability levels, preparation for the Spanish General Equivalency Diploma examination, and bilingual short-term intensive skill training supplemented with vocational English as a second language. A child drop-off center is provided for parents participating in the skills center.

Personal-Social Development. Working with psychologists from the regional Santee-Wateree Mental Health Center, Sumter Area Technical College in South Carolina provided a short course for police and sheriff's department line officers on coping with stress. More than seventy-five officers in four counties participated in the program, which enabled them to recognize and deal with stress in general as well as with job-related stress.

Clackamas Community College's (Oregon) Confidence Clinic is a structured ten-week program primarily for individuals who are experiencing a transition in their lives because of divorce, separation, death, or changes in their traditional roles. Self-improvement, self-awareness, and social independence are stressed through education, training, and counseling. The clinic provides the environment for the personal growth and the awareness of one's capabilities that form the foundation for self-confidence.

GTE Sylvania has contracted with North Shore Community

College, Massachusetts, to present a series of one-day retirement seminars for GTE employees and their spouses. The first of these "Planning for the Future" seminars was held in the spring of 1980; over one hundred persons participated in the workshops, which stressed preretirement planning in such areas as health care insurance, physical fitness after fifty, legal affairs, housing alternatives, and financial issues.

Family-Marital Relationships. Los Angeles City College sponsors a community-oriented workshop entitled "Parenting by Adoption," which offers basic information about the changing picture of adoption. The workshop helps its members decide whether adoption is for them. Social workers and adoptive parents (singles and couples) share their experiences and answer questions relating to adoption. Topics covered by the workshop include a list of the adoption agencies in the Los Angeles area and what they have to offer; independent and intercountry adoption; what to expect as one goes through the adoptive process; what children are waiting for families of their own; how experienced adoptive parents have dealt with older, emotionally or physically disabled children; the controversy over opening sealed adoption records; the search for family being conducted by some birth parents and some adult adoptees. An adoptive parent coordinated the workshop.

Borough of Manhattan Community Colleges (New York) Job Assistance Project for Battered Women provides job-readiness skills and job-placement assistance to economically disadvantaged women who have been the victims of domestic assault. The aim of the program is to help abused women become financially independent by providing the counseling, placement, and support services needed to obtain regular employment.

The Parent Resource Program is a parent education and enrichment program sponsored jointly by Manatee Junior College, Florida, and the School Board of Manatee County. Qualified instructors teach a variety of skills that enable parents to strengthen family relationships and to help develop their child's full learning potential. The program offers classes, workshops, seminars, and discussion groups in such areas as family communication, methods of discipline, single parenting, reading-readiness activities, learning activities to use in the home, and infant stimulation.

Citizenship. What constitutes a binding contract? Do "squatter's rights" still exist as a threat to property ownership? These and other legal questions were explained as six Richmond attorneys from the Young Lawyers section of the Virginia State Bar Association presented a well-attended lecture series on "Law Everyone Should Know" at the Parham Road Campus of J. Sargeant Reynolds Community College. Open to the public free of charge on successive Monday evenings, the lectures covered such topics as contracts, domestic relations law, real estate, wills and estates, accidents and liability, and criminal law.

Kirkwood Community College's "You and Your Community" is a seven-week course designed to give newcomers and others an in-depth introduction to the culture and heritage of Cedar Rapids, Iowa. In two-hour class sessions, the course deals with the city's history, education system, health services, arts, city government, and social services. Classes meet in locations throughout the city, and a variety of governmental and agency leaders serve as resource persons.

Kellogg Community College's (Michigan) "Building a Better Board" program has grown out of a community need to strengthen citizen boards. Seminar participants work together to examine such local needs as: (1) creating better relationships with other agencies to improve life in the community; (2) improving relationships among board members; (3) establishing better communications with administrators; (4) involving inactive board members; (5) utilizing the skills and talents of board members; and (6) attracting new, effective board members from the community.

The Center for Urban-Metropolitan Development of Cuyahoga Community College, Ohio, has "purchased" portions of different full-time faculty members' course loads to allow them to assist neighborhood groups in development. A computerized system for using the expertise of different faculty and community members is being developed.

Physical Environment. Marin Adventures, an outdoor education program sponsored by the Marin Community Colleges, is a single-parent-oriented weekend experience, providing instruction in outdoor skills (such as mountaineering or cross-country skiing), environmental issues, natural history, and local history. Each weekend course contains some exposure to biology, geology, history, and family-oriented recreation.

The Talking Garden is a prototype garden for handicapped persons conceived and developed by a visually handicapped community member, Norton Mason, Jr., at the Parham Road Campus of J. Sargeant Reynolds Community College. His Talking Gardens Foundation of Virginia, with help from the Kiwanians, the Telephone Pioneers of America, the college itself and others, has created a half-acre plot with aromatic and textural plants as well as vegetables and fruits to be enjoyed by blind and other physically or mentally handicapped persons. Some plants grow at ground level; some are raised for the convenience of persons in wheelchairs. The gardens are intended to inspire the handicapped to plant and care for their own gardens.

Fine Arts. The Alan Short Center of San Joaquin Delta College, California, originally opened with funding from private sources plus a state grant. The center's objectives are: (1) to use training in the arts as a vehicle to help neurologically and other handicapped students interact effectively with the environment; (2) to tap the creative and artistic potential of students in order to build self-confidence and to overcome historic patterns of failure; and (3) to present artistic, musical, and dramatic performances to the community to overcome misconceptions regarding handicapped individuals among members of the general public.

Florida Junior College (FJC) at Jacksonville has established the Women's Poetry Collective to encourage and promote an appreciation of poetry as an art form and to provide an outlet for women's creative expressions and perspectives in a changing society. A major project of the Women's Poetry Collective is a publication entitled *Kalliope: A Journal of Women's Art.* The poetry collective grew out of FJC's nationally recognized Center for the Continuing Education for Women.

North Country Community College's (New York) Center for Adirondack Studies has three goals: (1) to develop academic programs in Adirondack studies; (2) to provide resources on folk culture to students of the Adirondacks; and (3) to enrich the Adirondack community by developing activities that celebrate Adirondack life. The center has developed an A.A. degree program in Adirondack studies and has developed resources and classroom modules for elementary and secondary schools. In terms of providing resources for students of Adirondack folk culture, the center has developed an archive of tapes and transcriptions of oral history and folklore interviews, has acquired historical documents and photographs dealing with the people of the Adirondacks, and has developed an artifact collection of the culture.

Philosophy. Philosophy, whose popularity in the college credit program depends on the vivacity and reputation of the instructor, takes on a new meaning when focused on contemporary problems and issues. For example, the course entitled "Perspectives," offered by the Marin Community Colleges' Emeritus College, presents the insights of the world's major religions and schools of philosophy on death and dying, and the search for meaning in life. Other community education philosophy courses cover Eastern religions and provide exposure to viewpoints that contrast greatly with the Western thought often stressed in the credit program.

"Fridays, Ten 'Til Two" at Anchorage Community College is an interdisciplinary series devoted to topics of contemporary concern primarily to women. Registration is handled personally by the public services personnel so that no intimidating registration lines are involved. The series, which offers variable amounts of credit in humanities, may be paid for by the week, enabling a number of women on limited income to participate. Two hours of presentation and discussion, an hour for a buffet luncheon, and an hour of lively arts presentations constitute the program each Friday for eight weeks. One series is presented each semester, always on a different subject chosen by past participants. Topics have included "All About Eve," "The World of Personal Finance," "Psychology of Wearing Rose-Colored Glasses," "The Emotions: Chaos or Control," and "The Continuing Revolution: Human Values, Community, and Technology."

Recreation. Project CALL (Communities Alive for Living and Learning) at Kishwaukee College, Illinois, is a model in rural community education development, using a community college as the major support base in cooperation with schools, park districts, village governments, and other agencies. The major goal is to assist three rural communities in developing their own delivery systems for recreational, educational, and cultural programs as well as human services. An important facet of the project is building skills of local people in needs assessment, the development and use of resources, programming, and evaluation. Currently, each community has a project council, has participated in training, has implemented programs and services for various ages, has increased use of school space and other community facilities, has secured local funding and the involvement of county agencies, and has either a part-time or full-time coordinator.

The Marin Community Colleges have been a leader in enriching conventional physical education programs with such arts as Hatha Yoga and Tai Chi along with ballet and modern jazz dance.

Conclusion

Community general education provides a unique opportunity for the community college to make a direct contribution to the revitalization of our democratic form of government. Our system of government requires an informed and educated citizenry, for the people possess the ultimate power. The needs of our nation and its citizenry continue to become more complex as a result of demographic expansion, the information explosion, and increased leisure time (to cite just a few factors). Community general education permits our citizens to broaden their interests and insights and thus reponds to their increasingly complex needs.

Directly controlled by its potential student clientele, the community college has a vested interest in designing and offering a program of study based on community needs and interests. These needs and aspirations may be classified in accordance with the taxonomy suggested earlier and may become the basis of a community general education action plan. Programs reported in each category represent prototype offerings.

The community college possesses a full-time faculty, highly qualified in the field of general education yet seldom utilized in community programs. Because of declining enrollment in traditional programs, full-time faculty resources are readily available and should be utilized in shaping and providing the community general education function of the community college.

In addition to earning a living, the citizens of our communities, who are the students of the community college, want and need the general skills and values necessary for living their lives in harmony with others. For, as Ralph Waldo Emerson noted in 1837, a man must be a man before he can be a good farmer or tradesman or engineer (Blackman and others, 1976).

References

Blackman, R., Armstrong, E., Conrad, C., Didham, J., and McKune, T. *The Changing Practices in Undergraduate Education.* Berkeley, Calif.: The Carnegie Foundation for the Advancement of Teaching, 1976.

Chambers, R. H. "Educating for Perspective — A Proposal." *Change,* September 1981, pp. 45–51.

Luskin, B. J., and Chappell, J. "Coastline Community College: An Idea Whose Time Has Come." *UCLA Educator,* Winter 1981, *21* (1), 52–59.

Reynolds, J. *The Comprehensive Junior College Curriculum.* Berkeley, Calif.: McCutchan, 1969.

Zoglin, M. L. "Toward a Theory of Pluralistic Decision Making in Comprehensive Community Colleges." Unpublished doctoral dissertation, Department of Education, University of California, Berkeley, 1979.

Ervin L. Harlacher is chancellor, Marin Community College District, Marin County, California.

How shall we relate to our global neighbors,
and for what purpose?

General Education Through International/Intercultural Dimensions

Maxwell C. King
Seymour C. Fersh

Most of us have learned from experience the wisdom of the well-known Chinese proverb that "a journey of 10,000 miles starts with a first step." But even more important than taking the first step is having a clear sense of purpose as to where you prefer to go and why. A less well-known Hebrew proverb alerts us that "if you don't know where you want to go, all roads will take you."

This presentation has two major parts: First, we will share the thoughts that have influenced our actions at Brevard Community College, and, secondly, we will give examples of what we have been doing along with recommendations. At Brevard, we did not start with a master plan. Almost all that has happened (and is happening) evolved from what the Japanese call "a strategic accommodation — an incremental adjustment to unfolding events. . .in a continuous dialogue, what in hindsight may be called 'strategy' evolves" (Pascale, 1982, pp. 115–116). Our purpose has been to understand the nature of our contemporary world and to discover what kinds of education are likely to enhance life.

B. L. Johnson, (Ed.). *New Directions for Community Colleges: General Education in Two-Year Colleges*, no. 40.
San Francisco: Jossey-Bass, December 1982.

What in the World Is Happening to Us? —
Implications for General Education

We believe that, to live effectively and affectively in our rapidly evolving global society, individuals need additional kinds of knowledge and creative ways of becoming more self-educating. Previously, little conscious thought was given to what should be included in general education; everyone knew that it was merely a matter of "common sense"— each newborn was inducted into an existing, relatively unchanging society. What needed to be known was already known. The process of education was really one of training—the learner was encouraged and enjoined to follow the ways of the elders: priests, parents, professors, and patriarchs. This system works very well as long as two conditions exist: that there are few modifications in the society (in ideas and livelihood) and that a person remains in the same place.

Now and increasingly, the opposite conditions are true—few, if any, places are escaping rapid changes, and fewer people die in the same location where they were born. (Even if they stay in that place, the place itself is not the same.) These new conditions create human needs, one of which is that we must develop better foresight into the change to come as well as maintain our capacity to adapt and adjust to new situations.

These changes are, or course, related to others. Consider, for example, two developments that directly relate to general/international education and the community colleges: the rapid and dramatic increase in the United States in the number of foreign students and in the number of tourists. Foreign students' enrollment in the United States has increased from 9,600 students in 1930 to about 300,000 presently, and it is likely to be almost one million by 1990. If so, then foreign students may account for about 10 percent of all students in American colleges, compared with 2.7 percent in 1981 (Scully, 1981). The percentages for community colleges may be even greater because proportionately larger numbers of foreign students have been choosing our institutions. The present total is about 50,000.

Regarding our foreign tourists, the increases are even more dramatic. Such visitors were relatively rare until the mid-1970s; in 1982, the total number exceeded 23 million, and they spent $11.7 billion. For the first time, the number of incoming visitors is greater than the number of Americans going abroad. Tourism now ranks fourth as an American "export," that is, it provided a $300 million foreign currency surplus within an overall record of $40 billion balance of deficit payments in 1981. As part of our general education, Americans need to know that one in six of our jobs is related to international trade and that one of each three farm acres produces for export.

What Is Happening to the World? —
Further Implications for General Education

Until recently, what humans believed about themselves was largely a matter of personal choice. "Know thyself" has been urged upon us for over two thousand years, mainly on a take-it-or-leave-it basis. In other words, individuals who lived "reflective lives" presumably gained; those who did not were losers, but their loss did not threaten others. But times have changed. In this century, the human observations from the moon have helped confirm in a visual way what technology and ecology have been establishing in reality: that the human species now lives in the equivalent of a global village in terms of survival and fulfillment. Ethnocentric attitudes, appropriate, perhaps, in a tradition-directed society, provide too narrow and limiting a perspective in a global society.

Moreover, anyone whose life is restricted to knowledge only of his or her country does not share in the legacy of humankind. For Americans, the loss through lack of knowledge may be more than personal; it may be a loss for people in all parts of the world, since we are involving ourselves, through our government and commerce, in the affairs of others.

American achievements and ideals have enriched the world. We have done much of which to be proud. So have others. But our wisdom and actions must now include an awareness of how we affect others and are affected in turn. A better understanding and recognition of the interrelatedness of the human family and ecology are now essential.

What is urgently called for is an "adstructuring" of our perspectives — *ad* rather than *re*. We can benefit from the Hindu way of thinking that allows one to add perspectives without substituting them for earlier ones. And this adstructuring need not be an "agonizing reappraisal" but a joyful one. We can be elated because our world is so rich in talents and materials.

To add to our perspectives is not as difficult as it may seem at first. The ways in which we view the world, other people, and ourselves are, after all, the result of training and education, formal and informal. Humans are not born with perceptions; we learn them.

The Special Responsibility of Community Colleges

Within a global society, Americans must provide leadership and examples of good neighborly behavior. And within the United States, no institutions have a greater responsibility and opportunity to provide these services than do our community colleges.

These institutions are constantly innovating and developing. For example, until the 1970s, few of our more than 1,200 institutions gave much attention to curriculum matters or technical assistance that affected people and places beyond the local community. Increasingly, in the past decade, some community colleges have begun to broaden the definition of "community" to include the world community. This added perception was motivated in many ways — sometimes when foreign companies moved into the community or local businesses began overseas sales; sometimes when foreign students enrolled in the colleges; and sometimes when local educators modified the curriculum to include studies of an international dimension.

Our institutions also responded to leadership from other sources. In 1978, at the annual conference of the American Association of Community and Junior Colleges, the United States Commissioner of Education Ernest Boyer called upon our colleges to lead the way in rebuilding our commitment to international education, one that gives us a clear vision of the unity of our world. He concluded that he is convinced that our community colleges can and must take the initiative on this crucial agenda.

The Example of Brevard Community College

At Brevard Community College (BCC), leadership comes from both the ability to lead as well as to follow the administration and the faculty. For example, the coauthors of this chapter represent two major aspects of this institutional relationship: The president establishes the official commitment to the philosophy and implementation of particular institutional objectives; the coordinator of curriculum development works on the student/faculty/community level to enhance those programs that come into being and to help initiate others. There is also continuous participation in decision making at all levels; for example, the provosts at our three campuses are directly involved (as are division chairpersons) in selecting faculty for overseas assignments and for domestic enrichment opportunities.

The president sets the general course upon which the college is embarked. In the college's most significant document, its catalogue, the brief "President's Message" welcomes the students with these words: "Brevard Community College is your place to begin...to learn from and contribute to our growing, progressive institution, our community, and to our world" (p. 5). A few pages later, the following statement appears:

It is the policy of Brevard Community College to encourage and support the development of the many aspects of international/intercultural education. These would include (1) a structured process for the involvement of the community and the college; (2) study-abroad programs; (3) the internationalizing of the curriculum; (4) proper and effective programming of international students on campus; (5) programs of an international/intercultural nature for the community; (6) student, faculty, and staff exchange programs; (7) consultant and support services with foreign institutions; and (8) staff and program development activities [p. 9].

Having declared these international/intercultural purposes and intentions, the administration follows through with appropriate kinds of actions. For example, the president conveys the benefits of transcultural education by using existing opportunities (such as having a foreign educator as the graduation speaker) and creating new opportunities (such as a twice-a-year community dinner, when community as well as college members are invited to meet with foreign students). In addition, Brevard has helped create and belongs to consortia such as the International/Intercultural Consortium of the American Association of Community and Junior Colleges, the Florida Collegiate Consortium for International/Intercultural Education, and the College Consortium for International Studies.

Of special relevance is our membership in the Community Colleges for International Development (CCID); since its beginning in 1976, Brevard has provided its chairman of the board of directors and its executive director. The CCID provides a great variety of ways to encourage faculty development: It sponsors an annual conference that is attended by community college teachers and administrators from all over the United States; it provides overseas faculty exchanges with countries such as the Republic of China; it cosponsors conferences with international agencies such as the Organization of American States; it works with governments such as Surinam to strengthen development projects; and it directs its own summer program at the University of Konstanz in West Germany.

The Brevard administration also supports the college's general education goals by providing staff time and funds so that Brevard can apply and qualify for grants like those available from the federal government. For example, Brevard received a two-year grant in 1978 from the Undergraduate International Studies Program, which provides funds for the development of international dimensions in the general education curriculum. Likewise, it has received a grant for the past four years from the Foreign Curriculum Consultant Program, under which consultants have come from Brazil, Guatemala, Egypt, and the Gambia.

An additional way of strengthening faculty capability is through selective hiring. For example, a new instructor in our English department is from India; he teaches some of the regular courses and has initiated new courses (such as Hindi and Indian studies) as well as being an overall transnational consultant.

The administration also encourages and facilitates intercultural/international encounters and exchanges. For example, Brevard is often visited by foreign educators. In April of 1982, five college presidents from India were on campus for almost a week. In 1981, Brevard provided on campus a six-week management institute for seventeen administrators of technical schools in Surinam. Visits from international delegations are frequent; other countries represented have included Egypt, Jordan, Czechoslovakia, Zambia, Korea, Mauritius, United Kingdom, Australia, Canada, and Fiji. When these visits occur, opportunities are provided for our students and faculty to learn from the visitors as well as to provide educational services to them. These educators, among others, will soon benefit from the opening on campus of the International Foundation House, which will provide four guest rooms and a conference/reception room. The estimated cost of $50,000 for construction was raised by the BCC foundation through donations of cash, building materials, and construction skills.

Foreign student enrollment at Brevard is welcome and has occurred in relatively large numbers. In 1982, the total was about 350 students representing about forty countries and twenty languages. Over a third of the total is enrolled in engineering and about a fifth in business and commerce; and their primary source of funding is about evenly divided between their home governments and personal or family sources. This enrollment results not from active overseas recruitment, but, rather, because Brevard offers appropriate curricula, personalized counseling, and an overall environment (including its natural beauty) that is attractive and supportive. Innovative courses are especially designed to enroll local and foreign students in the same classes so that cultural encounters and shared experiences occur.

The foreign students are a valuable human resource for the college and community. From the office of the international division, appropriate arrangements are made to have these students help with such transnational needs as translating, tutoring in languages, travel suggestions, and general information. They also give talks and meet with community groups and with students in Brevard county schools as well as at the college.

In contrast to those policies and actions best initiated and implemented by the administration, there are other international/intercultural dimensions at Brevard initiated by the faculty. The most successful example is our Study Abroad Programs for students. These programs were first offered in the early 1970s by individual teachers who usually took groups of eight to ten students. The program began to expand rapidly in 1977 when 95 students went abroad; the major reason for the expansion was that one faculty member had gone abroad as a student in 1976 and was so stimulated by the experience that he has been organizing Brevard's programs ever since. He is the vitalizing force in a program that sends more than 300 students overseas annually; last year, students participated in five courses in Europe and two in Asia, and these also involved about twenty Brevard teachers and administrators.

Another good example of faculty involvement is represented by the teaching modules that were written as part of a federal grant for internationalizing the curriculum. A selection of these instructional units appears in the publication *The Community College and International Education: A Report of Progress* (Fersh and Fitchen, 1981). This 334-page publication consists of two parts: a collection of articles related to policies and programs in community colleges plus modules that were developed at selected institutions, including Brevard.

Leadership and responsibility for implementing the federal grant for the undergraduate international studies program came from our international studies division. It administers four major program areas: international studies, foreign languages, English for speakers of other languages, and counseling of foreign students.

The international division also initiates new courses that are especially designed to encourage and facilitate transcultural education among local foreign students. For example, in 1982 a course titled "Introduction to International/Intercultural Studies" attracted about eighty students, about a fourth of whom were from other countries; many of the other students were those who had been in the study abroad program.

This division has also increased the overall involvement of faculty and administration by creating, distributing, and administering its "International Education Questionnaire." Respondents were able to indicate their interests and capability for activities including the following: participating in workshops, conferences, and institutes; hosting international students and visiting educators; teaching, studying, and/or leading study groups abroad; and writing, reviewing, and/or presenting instructional or research materials. While the division does not centralize international/intercultural dimensions at Brevard, it does make special and significant contributions to overall developments.

Observations and Recommendations

From reading what has occurred at Brevard, one can deduce certain kinds of observations and recommendations: First, it is imperative that American educators (along with others) understand and appreciate the critical relationship of transcultural education and general education. We owe it to ourselves and to our global neighbors to become (in the words of the Dalai Lama of Tibet) "wise selfish"—that is, to realize that it is in our own interests to have consideration for others and to celebrate our membership in the human community.

General education of the kind we have been exploring is best advanced without a "strategic master plan." What we are doing at Brevard cannot serve as a prescription for others, but it can stimulate and encourage. Our experience is that one must have a will for there to be a way and that, complementarily, where there are ways, there are wills. When purposes and motivations change, problems can become opportunities—for example, an American "problem" has been the failure to appreciate properly the enrichment and stimulation that our ethnic differences have contributed to the mosaic of our culture.

Faculty development is, of course, directly related to curriculum development. Some would say that the faculty *is* the curriculum. In our approach to general education, the faculty is especially crucial because we have not chosen to achieve our purposes by requiring specific content-centered courses. Rather, we are affecting the curriculum (especially in the non–social studies courses) by increasing the number of faculty members with meaningful transcultural study and experiences. We do not require that faculty leaders of student study programs abroad be experts in the areas to be visited; we do require that they be well aware of our educational purposes for such programs.

General education generally has been considered to include all of those things that a person needs to know. Each culture has insisted that its own code of behavior was not only appropriate locally but also to be equated with "natural"; by inference, other cultures behaved unnaturally. General education increasingly will have to include an awareness that one's behavior is personal rather than universal and that the process of learning is more essential than mastery of content.

General education must be more concerned with the affective as well as the cognitive. Content-centered learning has relied heavily on accuracy and literalness at the expense of style and persuasive power; it increases "knowledge" of many things but not often at the feeling level, the level that excites one and makes one *care*. Learning should not, of course, exclude cognitive understanding, but it can and should communicate on levels other than the strictly intellectual.

When Confucius was asked what was the first thing he would do if he became the head of state, he said: "I would call things by their right names." What we have been calling "education" has been mainly "training"—learning what is already known. It makes sense to say that one received his or her training at such-and-such a place, but what are we implying when we say that the person *received* an education?

We will increasingly need (and should be glad) to become our own teachers in a world where educated selves can continue the process of self-educating. No content can serve this purpose better than cultural encounters. The discovery of "self" is also the discovery of "other"; without the combination, training is possible but not self-educating. We will need to develop the capacity to learn *from* the world as well as *about* it. The contribution that learning about other peoples and cultures can make will be revealed not only by our increased knowledge and awareness of them, but also by our complementary insights into ourselves and all humankind. We will not only know but we will also perceive, feel, appreciate, and realize. Through involvement and purposeful study, we can be helped to develop desirable qualities of empathy, self-development, humility, respect, gratitude, honor, puzzlement, and an overall sense of what it is to be human.

References

Fersh, S., and Fitchen, E. (Eds.). *The Community College and International Education: A Report of Progress.* Cocoa, Florida: Brevard Community College, 1981.

Pascale, R. "Our Curious Addiction to Corporate Grand Strategy." *Fortune,* Jan. 25, 1982, pp. 115–116.

Scully, M. G. "One Million Students at U.S. Colleges, Triple Present, Seen Likely by 1990." *Chronicle of Higher Education,* Oct. 21, 1981, p. 1.

Maxwell C. King is president of Brevard Community College.

Seymour C. Fersh is coordinator of curriculum development at Brevard Community College.

The list of obstacles to general education is lengthy and
complex. In the face of such obstacles, is there hope for the
revitalization of general education?

Obstacles to General Education

Terry O'Banion
Ruth G. Shaw

Almost as soon as general education is mentioned, someone will begin to
list the reasons why it will never work. This phenomenon is unique to
general education; no one will readily tick off the obstacles to vocational
education or will even claim that beleaguered liberal education would be
a great idea if only it could be put into practice. Unfortunately, it is
much easier to list the barriers to general education in the community
college than to describe the factors that support the movement. The
driving forces often appear to be fragile balloons full of theoretical hot
air, while statements of the restraining forces are as precise, as pointed,
and as lethal as pins.

     Critics of general education charge that it has been a movement
propelled too often by soft-headed idealists with bleeding hearts. The
critics style themselves, in contrast, as pragmatists, and they point with
pride to the success of career education as a specific solution to a specific
problem. If believers in general education are ever to respond to their
critics, they must understand the nature of the obstacles that lie before
them.

     Many of the barriers to general education in the community col-
lege are intangible, despite the fact that they can be stated precisely.
These obstacles are powerful because they are rooted in the respective

B. L. Johnson, (Ed.). *New Directions for Community Colleges: General Education in Two-Year Colleges*, no. 40.
San Francisco: Jossey-Bass, December 1982.

histories and philosophies that undergird the general education movement and the community college institution. A related collection of impediments includes those pertaining to the organization and delivery of
general education. A third set of obstacles relates to community college
staff, while a fourth cluster of problems is tied to the characteristics of
community college students. External and societal forces comprise yet
another group of difficulties. Despite these formidable obstacles, the
quest for general education in the community college continues, as its
advocates explore new avenues to overcome old barriers.

Intrinsic Conflicts

The most powerful obstacles are always those will-o'-the-wisps
called ideas. Much of the reason for resistance to or lack of enthusiasm
for general education in the community college can be traced to a perceived conflict between the institutional philosophy and the historical
underpinnings of general education.

Access vs. Elitism. Like it or not, general education is frequently
confused with liberal education. This confusion results in the fairly
widespread belief that there is something at least vaguely elitist about
general education that makes it improper as a fundamental mission of
the community college. Proponents of the general education movement
face an audience that has grown accustomed to dividing the world of
credit courses into hemispheres of academic and occupational.

Furthermore, the community college prides itself upon its attention to and accommodation of individual differences, while general education is predicated on the notion of commonality of learning. It seems
only fair to observe that "democracy's college" should embrace the Jack-
sonian idea that all its students might benefit from some common learning, but perhaps the rub develops when the precise nature of that learning must be defined. A Jeffersonian elitism creeps into the educational
garden of equality.

Pragmatism vs. Idealism. From the outset, the community college movement has been a pragmatic one. It was a practical solution to a
practical problem, designed to bypass the theoretical, often impractical,
folderol of academe. It is a blue-collar college, without apology.

Little wonder, then, that the advocates of general education have
often been their own worst enemy. With their imprecise definitions and
ill-defined outcomes, the proponents have come across as soft-headed
idealists, and the community college has always detoured around soft-
headed idealists. General education has perhaps been too "general," or it
has been defined in terms of what it is not (for example, it is not liberal

education). For the notion of general education to strike a chord with community college leaders, it must be described in more pragmatic ways. General education is practical, but somehow it never comes out that way.

Impediments in Organization and Delivery

The intrinsic conflicts are difficult to confront in any systematic fashion. But the barriers present in the organization and delivery of general education in the community colleges are universal and more tangible.

Organization by Discipline. It is the rare community college that does not organize its faculty and its curriculum by traditional academic disciplines. Commitment to the discipline is unlikely to be dissipated significantly in such a setting, and such academic allegiances, rightly or wrongly, create barriers to the integrating notions of general education. Cluster organization and interdisciplinary curriculum certainly do not provide the only response to the general education question, but at least they circumvent the territorial barriers of the academic disciplines. If the structure is to remain the same, then general education leaders must go to extraordinary lengths to weave organization fabrics that support general education. An example is the Skills for Living Program at Dallas Community College.

Failure to Program. Related to discipline organization is the failure of community colleges to plan, support, or evaluate their general education programs. In fact, most community colleges do not have anything that could properly be called a general education "program." When no one is in charge and no one has a vested interest, a monumental effort is required to design, offer, and evaluate such a program. The signal success of career education programs is in no small way related to the comprehensive way in which they have been developed. Certainly, the career education movement has been propelled by federal and state dollars, but it has also been characterized by careful design and evaluation related to the achievement of program goals. Even if the overall organization of the community college does not change, the nonchalant attitude toward programming for general education must.

Curriculum. The community college curriculum, forged from industry-required occupational courses and university-accepted academic transfer courses, and tempered by the 1960s' demands for student relevance, has been essentially closed to an intrusion of general education. The rise of vocationalism requires little elaboration. Perhaps the most pervasive value of American society is that human beings are not human beings unless they work and earn their way. This value under-girds the development and well-supported program of vocational educa-tion in the nation's community colleges. Current student attitudes re-flect the acceptance of this value as thousands rush, not to seek higher learning, but to attain job skills.

Vocationalism in itself is not an obstacle to general education, but the argument that all curriculum time must be devoted to vocational preparation for today's highly specalized jobs certainly is. There simply is not an opportunity for general education in the crowded curriculum of today's occupational student.

Not as often articulated is the point of view of many vocational educators who speak with disdain about the value of general education concepts: "Well, do you think a person ought to be able to listen to an opera or make a living?" Such views make further discussion hopeless.

The transferable portion of the community college curriculum has often been designed with the sole criterion of transfer in mind. Such an approach results in a course-by-course patchwork that gives a pass-ing nod, at best, to the integrating themes of general education. The as-sociate's degree is seen only as a step toward the bachelor's, not as the culmination of any activity that can and should have meaning it itself.

A final curriculum barrier to community college general educa-tion is the remnant of the "relevant curriculum" of the 1960s. As the stu-dents voiced it, education was meaningful only if they decided what it should be and only if it had some immediate and apparent personal ap-peal to them. The curriculum that students chalked on the walls or lob-bied for in corridors has long outlived its "relevance" in many instances. But the creative and intriguing curriculum variations of the 1960s dealt a near-fatal blow to the carefully conceived general education core cur-ricula of the 1950s. General education has never made a complete recov-ery from the devastation.

Identification with Personal Development. The personal devel-opment course is the bellwether of the general education movement. Many colleges in the 1950s and early 1960s included courses such as "Life Adjustment," "Orientation," or simply "Personal Development," which were often required for entering students. Although well in-tended and often well conceived, they were frequently failures in prac-tice. Few staff members were trained in human development, humanis-tic psychology, or group process. Thus, the courses often deteriorated into sophomoric attempts to teach students how to study or how to use the college resources. Efforts to encourage students to explore values or to make personal choices were often met with great ridicule because the lack of instructor competence resulted in shallow exercises. The courses were regarded as "easy A's" that lacked both substance and integrity. The advent of scientific education, which accompanied the launching of Sputnik, squashed the growth of the personal development movement, although it re-emerged as human development education in the late 1960s.

Unfortunately, the disdain for personal development education has transferred itself, by association, to general education. The basic suspicion that general education courses are academically soft is a barrier that has its roots in this old association. The relationship with human development education is a legitimate one, but some new and successful models must be developed if such courses are to be credible and respected.

Alliance with a Methodology. Another alliance that has become a hindrance for general education is that with process or methodology. A number of early leaders in general education said that it had more to do with a way of teaching than with course content. Viewing general education as a new way of teaching shows the difficulty of defining what it is. If it is a new way of teaching—for example, bending the subject matter to the student, rather than the student to the subject matter—then it will be difficult to design general education programs that will garner the support of those faculty members who do not favor this methodological approach.

Proponents of general education have encouraged contract grading, discussion groups, role playing, individualized study, self-grading and reporting, and wiping out the F grade. General education thus appears for many to be "progressive education" in a new disguise. Other curricular "movements," such as liberal education or career education, are not aligned with any particular methodology or approach to instruction and thus are spared the jousts with those who may support the concept but dislike the recommended methods.

Failure to Design Innovative Programs. Despite their well-deserved reputation for innovation, community colleges generally have been unsuccessful in designing programs of general education different from those of the senior institution. This failure presents at least two obstacles: It shows evidence of the failure to rethink general education for the community college context, and it lends credence to the criticisms of general education as elitist university bunk.

Certainly, there are notable exceptions in this widespread failure to design programs of general education especially for community college students, but even where community colleges have made concentrated efforts to design programs for their students, they have frequently been unable to move beyond the tried-and-true university models. The university models were, by and large, designed for homogeneous populations of resident students, and these models do not lend themselves easily to the heterogeneity of the community college.

Staff as Obstacles

The caring, creative staff of community colleges will be the key to success for general education. But staff members also present a variety of barriers to the general education movement.

Threat of Change. For most community colleges, the development of a bona fide general education program, organized around general education goals, would represent a radical departure from the traditional list of courses, which are required for reasons that may have been long forgotten. Any major change will meet with resistance in an organization, and few changes will meet with greater resistance in a college than changes to the curriculum.

In times of tightening resources, faculty are understandably skittish when course requirements are altered. The threat of shifting enrollments and the accompanying effect on job security is never forgotten during the lofty debates over general education. Some colleges have coped successfully with such fears by promising that no faculty member will lose his or her position as a result of changes to the general education curriculum, but not all institutions can hold out such promises. It is not only difficult but, perhaps, antithetical to basic human drives to put the greater educational good above the need for a regular paycheck.

Need for Staff Development. When faculty and staff are not openly resistant to general education programs, they may be indifferent, at best, or totally uninformed and unprepared, at worst. Yet seldom do well-designed staff development programs accompany new or revised general education plans. Thus, even well-conceived general education programs can fail quickly when faculty members are unable to teach them successfully. The problem here is clearly related to the resources of time and money. Few institutions are willing to devote the hours and dollars that it takes to ready faculty and other staff to conduct a general education program when it is assumed that "anyone" or "everyone" can handle general education.

Lack of Faculty Leadership. Faculty, preoccupied with career programs, their own disciplines, problems of remediation, or securing their positions, have exerted little leadership in the revitalization of general education. In some instances, administrators have usurped the faculty curriculum prerogative. In any case, general education in the community college has frequently found itself a cause without a champion. The challenge of inviting faculty to think about the educational issues related to general education and to design programs to address these issues is a major one for community colleges.

Lack of Administrative Support. Administrative support and educational leadership, essential to the success of general education, have been in short supply as management-oriented leaders have been preoccupied with enrollments, facilities, budgets, and political pressures. Many community college presidents today are selected for their managerial, rather than their educational, abilities. Such leaders, while necessary and effective in the settings in which they find themselves, are poorly prepared in terms of attitude or education to provide guidance for the general education movement. Yet such guidance and support is critical. In those few community colleges that have developed substantive general education, the president has been a central supporting leader. The lack of such support is a major obstacle to general education.

Students as Obstacles

It is perhaps ironic that the very students whom general education is meant to serve can also be seen as obstacles to it. But to ignore the barriers to general education presented by the characteristics and attitudes of community college students is to ignore also those traits that successful general education programs must be designed to accommodate.

Heterogeneity. The very heterogeneity of the student population upon which the community college prides itself presents serious problems in the development of general education or "common learning." General education is predicated upon the basic assumption that certain learning should be common to all people; it focuses upon the connectedness of things. But when the student population varies in age, preparation, ability, experience, and interest to the extent that the community college population varies, it is difficult to discern a common point of departure, much less to establish the learning that should be common to all students. Once the task of identifying the common ground is accomplished, however, one is still faced with the problem of how to reach it.

Attendance and Motivation. If one were to consider attendance patterns alone, one would face a considerable barrier to general education in the community college. The students are increasingly part-time, on campus only for one or two courses taken in a frequently random sequence. They drop in for one semester and stop out for two. They attend in the evening and may complete their community college degrees without ever encountering a full-time instructor.

Their reasons for attendance present yet another obstacle. They are enrolled for a few courses to upgrade their job skills. They want to attain entry-level occupational skills as quickly as possible (read that to mean "without taking all that general education junk"). They just plan to take one or two courses for personal improvement. They intend to satisfy their general education requirements at the university when they transfer.

On top of this barrier, roll out the concertina wire: They could not care less about ever receiving the associate's degree. Either they plan to pursue a bachelor's, so it doesn't matter, or they plan to get a job, so it doesn't matter. The age-old collegiate weapon of "It's required for your degree" simply won't cut it with today's community college students. *You* can require it for *your* degree all you want; it is simply not in their plans.

Wherefore the core? Wherefore required courses? Wherefore general education? The initiation of the Miami–Dade general education program, which is built around a carefully designed core, may provide a partial answer to these questions. Meanwhile, any plan for general education must take factors of student attendance and motivation into careful consideration.

Failure to Include Basic Skills. Although community college students often lack the basic skills in reading, writing, and computation, most general education programs have failed to integrate or even address the issue of basic skills training. Even if all the resources were present, even if faculty and administration strongly supported general education, even if the effects of philosophical impact could be negated, the basic skills problem would remain. How should basic skills be incorporated into general education? Or should they be at all? How can students benefit from the values of a general education program when they cannot read or write? Colleges have designed remedial and developmental programs to cope with the basic skills problems, but these programs are seldom integrated with or even connected to a program of general education.

Attitudes. Student attitudes, including resistance to curriculum prescriptions and an overweening vocationalism, are not supportive of general education programs. Students tend to see many general education programs as denying them their inalienable rights to select the content and sequence of their educational programs. They believe that their vocational goals will not be achieved if they have to take required courses that do not appear to relate to their immediate needs. The resistance to general education requirements is so widespread and so fundamental that we have come to see it as natural and to be expected. It is an attitudinal barrier comparable to that of faculty resistance to curriculum change.

External and Societal Restraints

American society includes forces that drive us toward general education and equally powerful forces that inhibit its growth in the nation's educational institutions. The restraining forces are many; a few of the most potent ones are examined here.

Specialization. America has become a nation of specialists, partly at the behest of the educational system, which now decries the lack of support for general education. The nation has thrived, in part, because of its emphasis in the professions on specialization. When not only institutional policies and procedures but also the entire society are designed to encourage specialization, how can general education fit into the plans?

The "Me Generation" and the "Moral Majority." The advent of the "me generation" has gnawed at the very foundation of general education: that is, the idea that there are common links that bind humanity. And it has eroded the fundamental principle upon which general education is based: that a common core of social values exists. When an entire generation devotes itself to narcissistic self-indulgence, how can the value of a general education be translated? If, as some behavioral scientists avow, there is no longer a core of values in American society, what will be the basis of general education, which has heretofore been in great part designed upon such a core?

The opposite face of the "me generation" is found in the "new right," equally a societal obstacle to general education in its prescriptive moralism and rigid doctrines. If the narrowly defined values of the new right are confused with the common core of values espoused by general education, then general education may be associated with the same sort of intellectual dwarfism that has characterized this movement. A more blatant obstacle to general education is apparent in the opposition of the new right to the liberating, humanistic philosophies that have long undergirded the general education movement.

Focus on Survival. The emergence of the "me generation" is related to the social emphasis on survival in recent years. A declining economy, rising crime, and dwindling natural resources have focused educational and public attention on survival strategies, not on areas perceived as esoteric. General education, unfortunately, has too often been viewed as nonessential and esoteric, several steps up the hierarchy from survival. Proponents argue loudly, but not too effectively, that general education values are more important than ever when we must cooperate in order to survive. General education could shine in this arena, but the connections must be presented more effectively to students and to community constituents.

External Control of Curriculum. Community colleges have been particularly susceptible to control of their general education curricula by external agencies such as senior colleges, occupational advisory boards, and state agencies. Even though the majority of community college students do not transfer to the universities, community colleges still respond to university control on courses to be transferred. In some states, university requirements actually dictate the basic general education core for a community college.

Some hope for improvement is held out by models such as the General Education Compact for the State of Florida, which ensures that a community college may develop its own general education program, print it in its catalogue, and be assured of its acceptance for transfer to any state university in Florida. Unfortunately, most community colleges continue to line up with the traditional requirements of the university.

Occupational advisory boards shape the curriculum most frequently by squeezing out general education courses to permit more vocational credits. State agencies, governing boards, and legislatures have also created barricades to general education in some cases. For example, Texas requires two courses in American history and two courses in government. This requirement leaves little room for imagination in the development of the social science dimension of a general education curriculum. With all of the internal problems that general education must face, the intrusions of external barriers add insult to injury.

Overcoming Obstacles

The sad thing about this chapter is that it is so easy to write. No assignment could be easier than ticking off the obstacles to general education. Far more difficult is the task of overcoming these obstacles. There are no easy solutions and no panaceas. Some of the barriers are fundamental; they simply form the parameters within which general education must function. The recent revival of interest in general education in the community college is clear evidence that the obstacles can be overcome and that the goal is worthy of the effort that is required. There are many avenues available to those committed to the revitalization of general education. A few of the more obvious ones are set out here.

Review of Goals and Methods. The goals and the delivery of general education programs are worthy of major review to assure that they are adapted to new times and a changed student population. The general education of today does not have to be synonymous with the general education of yesterday. Indeed, one of the definitions of general education is that it is the common learning for the common man in his or her time and place. We are in a different time and place than the 1950s, and the goals of general education should reflect that difference.

Even recently developed general education programs show little sensitivity to the characteristics of community college students. For example, most groups planning general education programs proclaim loudly that the program does not have to be limited to a core of courses. However, the result is invariably a core of courses—usually a predictable cluster of five or six requirements. This traditional model is perhaps unnecessarily limiting. If general education is conceived as a core of outcomes or experiences, rather than as a core of courses, then this core could be achieved through a variety of means more appropriate for the community college students of the 1980s. We have not even begun to tap the resources of instructional design and technology in the creative solution of general education programs. Individual assessment, cable television, learning units—all have possibilities in the delivery of meaningful general education.

Staff Development. Extensive, long-term, well-planned staff development can be an important contributing factor to the success of general education. Indeed, a report on the general education model at Los Medanos College goes so far as to say that "this project has demonstrated beyond question that the most important determinant of success in curriculum innovation is professional staff development" (Carhart, 1980, p. 8). Many of the obstacles outlined here can be addressed through a sound staff development program. In fact, when such staff development sessions are organized around general education issues, faculty members may find themselves, for the first time since graduate school (or perhaps for the first time ever) grappling with questions of educational philosophy and priority. Such a setting is stimulating and can revive not only general education but also the waning spirits of many a "burned out" faculty member.

Design of Alternate Programs. Because of the student diversity and the attendance patterns of the community college, general education programs for specific groups of students may need to be identified. While such a notion may seem antithetical to "common learning," it is predicated on the pragmatic view that some general education is better than no general education.

If it is impossible to develop an institution-wide program for all students, it may still be possible to develop general education programs for selected groups. Nursing students might follow a program with certain emphases, while business students and transfer students might follow other patterns. These alternatives could address common goals, but in ways tailored to the needs of the particular student groups. Such an approach has the added benefits of attracting greater faculty interest and of demonstrating the relevance of general education to students enrolled in the program.

Noncurricular Dimensions. Most discussion of general education is limited to the curriculum. However, there are many opportunities for general education that lie beyond the curriculum. Noncredit or community service programs could provide creative routes to the attainment of general education goals. Student development programs, wellness programs to prevent stress and disease, and other student services are tailor-made to meet many of the goals of general education. But it will take some imagination and ingenuity to make the connections to these noncurricular dimensions of the educational program.

One appealing possibility is the notion of a general education program for adults. General education is usually conceived as a program for the young or inexperienced. And yet, if it has a basic value and integrity, then all adults, even older adults, can probably see the value of general education in their lives.

The fifty-five-year-old business executive understands full well that she has missed out on the humanities. The thirty-seven-year-old salesman knows that he needs to sharpen his communication skills. The forty-five-year-old returning housewife is excited about the human development course that will allow her to explore various careers and value choices. Once adults have achieved their basic Maslovian needs, a college might advertise bluntly: "Do you feel the gaps in your education? Even though you have a college degree, do you feel educated? Are there courses you wish you had taken? Opportunities you wish you hadn't missed? Then come to your local community college to fill in the gaps, or just to stop and catch up. It's never too late to be an educated person."

Such a special program would necessarily explore noncurricular, as well as curricular, means for its achievement. But this kind of program would be designed for the times in which we live and for the particular kinds of people that we serve.

Need for Systematic Planning. If general education is ever to succeed in the community college, the same kind of programmatic planning, support, and evaluation that have characterized career and developmental programs must be committed to general education. A point of departure for such planning will be the identification of elements of general education that are in particular harmony with the community college philosophy and purpose. A fundamental adherence to democratic principles undergirds both movements, but this commonality is seldom explored. General education is a great equalizer and, as such, should have special appeal for "democracy's college." The spectre of elitism can be cast out by the recognition and articulation of such common principles.

Beyond this important step, however, colleges must commit the human and financial resources to general education that have been devoted without question to other dimensions of the curriculum. Responsibility for the success of the general education program must be fixed and must be shared by faculty and administration. Programs that are systematically designed must be systematically evaluated. And the experiences or courses in such programs must be the best that they can be, not the dregs of the institution, taught by junior instructors to jumbo classes of yawning students. All too often, general education cannot be described appropriately as a program at all. It is often merely a list of courses required by the nearest university, placed mindlessly, heedlessly, into the catalog. No wonder that it has been difficult to take it seriously.

Conclusions

General education is the best idea that ever came down the pike for community colleges. Critics would claim that it's the best idea that will never work. The obstacles outlined here will certainly make the weak of heart agree, for the obstacles are many and are pervasive. Some institutions will never develop a general education program worth its salt; most will not even try. But for those few brave, hardy, and healthy institutions that will make the attempt in this decade, we offer applause and encouragement. The community college of the future will survive without general education programs — but with them can come a liveliness, a coherence, an integrity, and an identity that marks the difference between survival and success.

References

Carhart, J. "A Report on the General Education Model of Los Medanos College." Unpublished manuscript, Los Medanos College, Pittsburg, California, 1980. (ED number not yet assigned.)

Terry O'Banion is vice chancellor of educational affairs for the Dallas County Community College District.

Ruth G. Shaw is associate vice-chancellor of educational affairs for the Dallas County Community College District.

*It is time for vigorous action, for the proponents of general
education to bring forth sound proposals — and produce
results. We have been handed the tools: fiscal retrenchment,
demands for quality, demands for excellence. We can create a
commitment to general education that will influence our future.*

General Education:
Challenges and Choices

Judith S. Eaton

The term "general education" may be used to refer to the development of
a wide range of skills that assist individuals in leading productive, meaningful, and humane lives in a complex social, technological, and cultural environment. It assists us in having careers, being scholars, falling
in love, having friends, being religious, and making money.

We in community colleges have tended to identify general education with a transfer or "personal interest" curriculum. We have not
identified it with technical education as represented by our associate or
applied science degrees. General education activity is sometimes identified with the liberal arts or humanities portion of the curriculum. We
might serve ourselves more effectively, however, if we were to place
more emphasis on the *goals* associated with general education rather than
on the curriculum used to achieve theses goals. General education refers
to competencies and skills gained through both technical and liberal arts
training — it is that which provides an individual with skills for earning a
living, caring about others, sharing in culture and values, contributing
to our world, and analyzing environment and existence.

When education at any level was conceived to be a "full-time"
activity, general education was frequently synonymous with fulfilling

B. L. Johnson, (Ed.). *New Directions for Community Colleges: General Education in Two-Year Colleges*, no. 40.
San Francisco: Jossey-Bass, December 1982.

degree requirements. Much of our concern about general education in today's community colleges surrounds the reality that our students are part-time, nondegree, and nongraduate. We have paid a price for the part-time student in commitment, investment, and valuing. When community college course work appears roughly synonymous with a trip to your local fast-food outlet for hamburgers, pizza, and eggs, little of value will happen. Higher education "worked" for full-time students *because* they made a major investment of time and money. While many of our part-time students are making a serious commitment of time, this commitment competes with many other obligations. Education in community colleges has become, for many, a peripheral activity. What happens to our commitment to general education under these conditions?

Urban four-year colleges and universities with strong undergraduate programs are in an increasingly strong position to do what community colleges claim to do. As resources tighten and institutional survival is at stake, more and more of these institutions will take on the trappings of community colleges. Many have already done so. We are seeing open admissions, increased emphasis on career education, catering to part-time students, fewer resident students, and a refashioning of the liberal arts curriculum at these institutions.

As we begin to experience a public policy that restricts support for education, we need to encourage general education by means of creative refashioning of existing resources rather than by acquiring additional money and support. This means that general education will be denied the benefit of strong external fiscal and psychological support. This means that fresh attention to general education will have to occur without augmentation or expansion of budgets, staff, and curriculum. This means that we will have to take a critical look at what we are doing and decide to refocus some of our energy and resources.

The situation might be viewed as an opportunity. Why should we maintain that all activities presently housed within our organizations are sacred and cannot be altered or removed? It will take astute management of resources to bring about redefinition and it will take pain, loss, anger, and conflict.

Challenges

Encouraging general education in community colleges requires attention to institutional goals, students, faculty, curriculum and instruction, academic standards, management and leadership, and external influences. This encouragement is not confined to some alteration in the instructional program or the initiation of special courses or services.

General education is not a *single* issue; rather, it involves a variety of existing college activities and commitments, as seen in Figure 1.

Institutional Goals. Most community college mission statements encourage general education. That is, they encourage broad-based learning, cultural connectedness, and development of various kinds of skills.

Does the structure of an institution provide for the achieving of these goals? Are staff appropriately selected and trained to achieve these goals? What is the impact of external constituencies? How do we achieve consistency of goal and effort?

Students. Recent data ("Retention and Transfer," 1980; Carnegie, 1979) indicate that students are in college for two major reasons: to obtain jobs and to make money eventually. While community colleges enroll students from ages fifteen to eighty, the modal age of these students is 21.5. It is the mean age (twenty-nine) that suggests, perhaps misleadingly, an older population (Cohen, 1981).

Today's students are part-time with academic skill levels from the remedial to graduate level. They are enrolled in various curricula that include "blue collar" technologies. They have many outside interests and responsibilities. They have been inundated with instructional technology reflecting increased emphasis on computers, video, and microelectronics. They seem to place limited value on course completion, are indifferent to grades, and see a limited relationship between education and jobs, education and money, education and success: the 1980s do not provide a context of optimism as did the 1960s.

Faculty. Among the challenges concerning faculty, not the least is the fact that there is less money. There are fewer jobs and a general decline of opportunity within and among institutions. Faculty are beginning to feel "stuck" in a given job (Connolly, 1981; Kanter, 1980). They, too, feel the impact of a loss of values and direction. They, too, lack the skills of prediction in a rapidly changing society. There is little about which they can feel certain. Public policy of the 1980s suggests that their work is less than valued and appreciated in our society.

Curriculum and Instruction. The curriculum of an institution is the product of many forces: faculty, administrators, boards, legislatures, "the community." It is in many ways the product of negotiation and compromise. Lack of consensus makes it difficult for faculty and management to work together in areas of curricular concern. It also makes it difficult for management to carry out an academic leadership role.

We still have a strong tendency to perceive our curriculum as though it were intended for a nonexistent student population. By identi-

Figure 1. General Education: Challenges

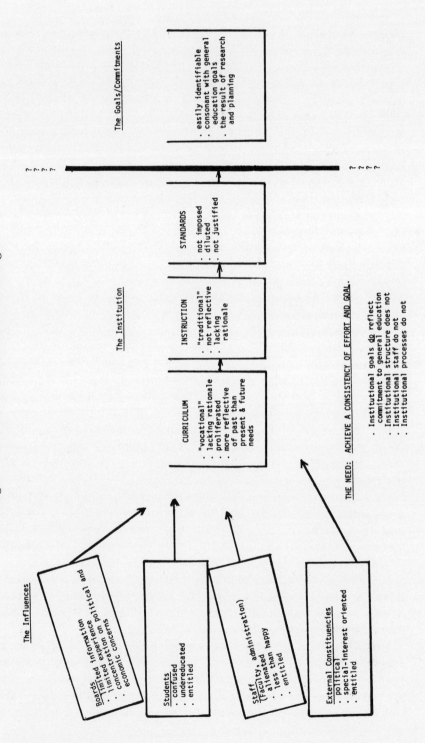

fying general education with distribution requirements associated with degrees, we have eliminated mandatory general education from a curriculum designed for a predominately nondegree clientele. Emphasis on training (versus education) has additionally diluted our general education commitment. The same is true for community college involvement in community service and other noncredit activity. There are those who identify general education with basic skill training or remedial education. Our challenge is two-fold: to clarify the relationship between faculty and management regarding curriculum responsibility and to develop curriculum such that general education is preserved in a part-time, nondegree, nontransfer context.

Academic Standards. Do we give too many A's and B's and too many marks? It is also possible that we have earned the disinterest and the disregard of employers, transfer institutions, and scholars. Is permissiveness a justification for failing to demand quality and to set expectation levels that require students to make a significant intellectual investment? The challenge here is to balance our demand for quality with our commitment to access.

Management and Leadership. The management challenge in encouraging general education requires attention to organizational structure, curriculum development, and staff development. It is a responsibility among many other competing and equally important responsibilities. Yet managers still possess a unique opportunity to set the academic value agenda for an institution.

We need to retain faculty as the chief architects of the curriculum while managers fulfill their obligation as leaders of vision (goal setters) and sources of primary support. Managers and faculty can work together to develop programs, methods, and values associated with the curriculum. If management provides a context for curriculum development and an environment of support, faculty can fulfill their key role of realizing general educational goals. When goals reflect strong commitment to general education, faculty are likely to move in this direction.

External Influences. General education curriculum might develop even without managers and leaders. Awareness on the part of boards and the community will not. Managers are challenged to educate boards and the community that the term "general education" is not a vague bit of jargon comprehensible only to educators.

Because of the scope and complexities of the changes we are experiencing, we have an unusual opportunity to gain community support for general education goals. Community leadership needs to see the great stake they have in general education and the value of community colleges as collegiate institutions. Boards, if they are particularly well informed about an institution's intent and direction, can assist in bringing about support for general education efforts. We need to educate those around us about a newly defined general education that is not identified only with the transfer curriculum. (The public is likely to see our institutions as vocational training centers without commitment to general education unless we have a transfer function — or a replacement for it.)

Choices

Importance of Institutional Goals. Institutional goals have particular viability when they are the product of consensus. Boards, the community, faculty, and students can be involved effectively in the development of the intent of an institution. In order that institutional goals reflect commitment to general education, it is important that the constituencies who help create these goals have before them the expected results of the efforts of an institution. It is one thing to develop nice-sounding statements to be placed in college catalogues: *it is another thing to develop a profile of skills one may reasonably expect a student to have—* whether part-time or full-time — in our institutions. Goals should be accepted or rejected based upon this profile.

Importance of Faculty. There was a time when staff development may have appeared to be an unnecessary indulgence on the part of institutions designed simply to placate faculty. Now, because of the maturation and the lack of mobility of faculty, staff development has become a major institutional investment in the future. The presence of long-term faculty in an environment of restricted resources and limited mobility (whether internal or external) suggests the need for staff development programs that can function as catalysts to produce needed change in approach and intellect. The staff development programs that already exist at many of our institutions can be molded to reflect an institutional commitment to general education.

Importance of Curriculum. Unless our student body magically alters to become predominantly full-time, it is critical that we clarify the role of general education as it relates to short-term training and part-time, nondegree students. If we adopt institutional general education goals, then all curricular adventures can be assessed for their general education effectiveness.

Importance of Academic Standards. We have an obligation to provide not only information and analysis but also to set standards. Our institutions simply do not possess the resources to educate all people under all conditions. We have been admitting as many people as possible and failing to assist a very high percentage of them. We need to face the reality that we have an obligation not only to students but also to student success. We need to face the reality that this success requires our commitment to public standards of quality. We need to face the reality that we can achieve these standards for a diverse student population only if we provide adequate support systems for the students we serve.

Management. Management is in a unique position to influence the direction of general education efforts. It is important, however, to go beyond good intentions and public identification with general education goals to specific management efforts that stress support for general education. Such efforts might include presenting management development workshops on general education or making stipends and adjusted course loads available to faculty and administrative teams for planning specific general education programs.

Importance of External Influences. "General education" is probably a less-than-meaningful term to the general public. A community relations effort could be launched that would provide definition and clarification. We need to overcome the apparent lack of specificity of the phrase by:

1. Pointing out to employees that the general skills they consider important (qualitative, quantitative, interpersonal, social) are available through general education efforts,
2. Taking the time to encourage understanding of the practical quality of general education to the community at large and state legislatures,
3. Identifying general education with quality and excellence as highly desirable educational goals,
4. Identifying general education with definition of social values and social commitment,
5. Creating, when appropriate, general education community task forces.

The encouragement of general education requires the successful meeting of challenges associated with our colleges, our communities, and our colleagues. There are many choices available to us; we have summarized some of them in Figure 2. It is most important to make decisions and take action—it is most important to ensure the effective survival of general education at our institutions.

References

Cohen, A. Remarks to the Northwest Association of Community and Junior Colleges, Portland, Oregon, December 1981.

Connolly, J. J. "Community Colleges in the 1980s." *Educational Record, 1981, 61* (4), 35–40.

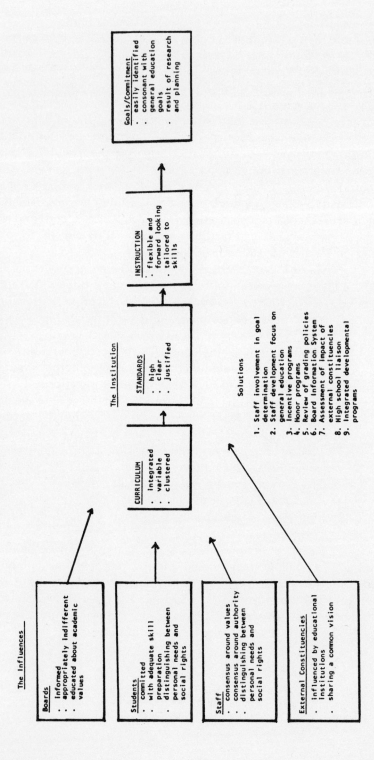

Figure 2. General Education: Choices

Kanter, R. M. "Quality of Life and Work Behavior in Academia." *National Forum,* 1980, *60* (4), 35–58.

Levine, A. "Today's College Students: Going First Class on the Titanic." *Change,* 1981, *13,* (2), 16–23.

"Retention and Transfer," *University of California Undergraduate Enrollment Study,* University of California, Berkeley, June 1980.

Judith S. Eaton is president, Clark County Community College, North Las Vegas, Nevada.

Launching a new general education program
requires careful planning, extensive faculty involvement,
and administrative support.

Getting Started:
Straightforward Advice

Jeffrey D. Lukenbill
Robert H. McCabe

During the past three decades, American community colleges have met admirably the challenge of providing expanded access to postsecondary education. They have developed new opportunities for individuals who had previously been excluded to receive the training and education necessary to participate fully in our society. The technical developments of American industry during World War II produced dramatic shifts in the mix of occupations. The number of unskilled jobs declined sharply while the number of skilled, semiprofessional, and professional jobs expanded sharply. These changes not only permitted more individuals to attain a higher economic status but also drastically increased the education required. The community college evolved to fill that requirement. Thus, these institutions became the principal vehicle of the "access revolution" that has since dominated American higher education.

Clearly, American higher education is in a period of transition. For more than thirty years, a basic concept of the community college has been to expand access. The opening of opportunity to new populations has been surprisingly successful. The access revolution, however, has also been a major contributor to a decline of standards. Community col-

B. L. Johnson, (Ed.). *New Directions for Community Colleges: General Education in Two-Year Colleges*, no. 40.
San Francisco: Jossey-Bass, December 1982.

leges have been too often more successful in enrolling new populations than in serving them effectively. The curriculum review process now under way in education is reflective of a pervasive public attitude that places major emphasis on quality, rather than on access.

Many who are concerned with improving the quality of postsecondary education offer a simplistic solution to the problem — that is, to limit admission to those demonstrating high ability on completion of high school. While raising admission criteria might be appropriate for certain universities, such a policy applied to all higher education would have a devastating negative impact on this country. American society and the American economy need more, rather than fewer, well-educated individuals.

It is time to examine carefully the current environment and to redesign realistically the postsecondary system, especially the community college, to become a positive force in improving our society. The combined effect of the changing nature of work in America, along with a severe decline in the communications skills of youth, have resulted in a societal dilemma so serious that it can be called a crisis. Quite simply, the increased requirement for academic skills for employability, combined with the decline in those skills among young Americans, leaves literally millions of Americans inadequately prepared and unable to gain employment and thus unable to sustain themselves as productive members of the society.

One area of critical importance in the renewal of community colleges is general education. To provide all individuals with the knowledge and skills they need in order to function in society, to find self-fulfillment, and to be prepared for lifelong education and a variety of careers, community colleges must develop challenging and effective general education programs. Career preparation, without broad academic skills, is insufficient.

General Education: Where to Begin?

Comprehensive Approach. An apparently logical starting point for a general education revision is the existing general education requirements. A college needs to identify those general education courses that are successful so that they can be used as models for other courses. But greater emphasis should be given to those courses and aspects of the general education requirements that are not so successful. These courses might have to be revised or new courses substituted for them.

This "praise the good" and "change the bad" approach is based on a fundamental assumption that there is a sound philosophical and educational basis for the existing general education requirements. If there is this foundation for the general education program, then the approach of identifying strengths and weaknesses in the program can be very effective. In fact, such a review should be ongoing so that regular revisions are made to account for changes in students' needs and for other external factors that influence the curriculum.

Unfortunately, most colleges do not have a sound foundation for their general education programs. A primary reason is that those colleges have general education *requirements* and not general education *programs*. A true general education program will have four essential components: (1) a rationale, (2) goals, (3) courses and objectives for attaining the goals, and (4) evaluation.

Before its general education study, Miami–Dade Community College (Florida), like most other community colleges, did have general education requirements — specific courses that students had to complete. The college did not have statements about why these courses were necessary, what they were to achieve, or what relationships existed among the courses. Neither faculty members nor students understood clearly why these requirements were imposed. Unless a college has this clear rationale for its general education program and general education goals, it should begin the review with fundamental questions.

Why Have General Education? A rationale for having a general education program will include explicit statements of the values that general education can provide. College administrators and faculty will have their own personal reasons for supporting general education, but the college as an institution needs to be explicit about its reasons. Miami–Dade identified five reasons why general education should benefit students (Lukenbill and McCabe, 1978):

1. A general education should enable individuals to integrate their knowledge so that they may draw upon many sources of learning in making decisions and taking action in daily practical situations.
2. A general education should provide students with a beginning or a further commitment to a lifetime of learning.
3. A general education should enable students to intensify the process of self-actualization.
4. A general education should enable students to find value in the activities and experiences of their lives, both those in which they engage because of obligations or commitments and those which are discretionary in nature.
5. Finally, general education should increase students' understanding of the breadth and depth of ideas, the growth of soci-

ety and institutions, and the development and application of the scientific process in communities throughout the world.

What Is General Education? It is important for a college to define general education for itself. The definition adopted by Miami–Dade stresses the integration of sources of learning in order to provide a basis for inquiry and decision making (Lukenbill and McCabe, 1978).

General education at Miami–Dade Community College is that aspect of the college's instructional program which has as its fundamental purpose the development and integration of every student's knowledge, skills, attitudes, and experiences so that the student can engage effectively in a lifelong process of inquiry and decision making [p. 29].

What Are the Goals of General Education? Some colleges have identified general education goals, but these goals have not been related directly to general education requirements and courses. Without general education goals, a college has no basis for determining whether the general education program is achieving what it was set up to accomplish. Miami–Dade's general education goals are grouped in six categories: (1) fundamental skills, (2) the individual, (3) the individual's goals for the future, (4) the individual's relationships with other persons and groups, (5) society and the individual, and (6) natural phenomena and the individual. The twenty-six goals in these groups were used to define five new core courses that are required for all degree students.

If a college can get agreement among faculty and administrators about general education goals, it can proceed with a substantial general education review. The college faculty can then address the next basic question: Through what curriculum structure can the majority of students best achieve these general education goals?

Administrative Content. A strong general education program should be at the core of the entire community college curriculum. General education goals usually apply to all degree-seeking students (although the kinds of requirements may vary for associate in arts and associate in science students). Consequently, changes in the general education program affect a majority of the faculty — if not the courses they actually teach, then the degree programs in which their students are enrolled.

Changes usually produce tension. When these changes directly affect faculty members' teaching assignments, the stress can be great. An environment of declining enrollments only serves to exacerbate the situation. In its general education study, Miami–Dade found that considerable tension developed between the faculty and administration, among campuses, among departments within a campus, and among faculty members themselves.

Any change that affects a college so extensively must have strong administrative leadership and support. Changes in the general education curriculum may affect the administrative organization of the curriculum and departments, the enrollment in specific courses, the security and comfort of faculty members, the priorities of the college's support services, and the students as they find themselves in the midst of changing requirements.

In anticipation of some of these tensions, the president, at the beginning of Miami–Dade's general education study, made the commitment that no faculty members would lose their jobs as the result of any changes in the general education requirements. Faculty members were certainly not guaranteed that their teaching assignments would remain the same, nor even that they would not have to change to some degree their teaching fields. It was clear from the beginning of the study that the addition or deletion of required courses would significantly impact the full-time equivalent (FTE) generated by those departments responsible for the courses. Some departments might well need fewer full-time instructors as the result of the deletion of a required course.

As part of the commitment to faculty, the president also agreed to provide faculty development programs and activities for those faculty members who might have to teach courses outside their immediate fields. This faculty development support was especially necessary for new interdisciplinary courses in the humanities and the natural sciences. Thus, from the beginning of its general education revision, Miami–Dade included plans for an integrated process of curriculum development and faculty development.

Faculty members who participate in general education steering committees, in course-development committees, and in the implementation of new general education programs have a special need for administrative support. For many of these faculty members, their participation is a new role. They find that their proposals and recommendations are open to critical review and attack by their peers. These faculty members need to know that their efforts are supported by the administration and, furthermore, that their recommendations result in action.

One major reason for the success of Miami–Dade's general education revision was the complete support of the president. The executive vice-president chaired the general education steering committee and facilitated the difficult process of initiating such a comprehensive review. A faculty member was released full-time to be the director of the study in order to plan the review process, provide background reading, arrange for nationally prominent external consultants, draft position papers, and ensure the necessary communication with the administrators and faculty on all campuses. This personal and economic support by the president and the executive vice-president was absolutely essential to the implementation of the general education reform.

Faculty Involvement. Although administrative support for a general education review is essential, it would be a serious mistake for a college's administration to try to impose a new general education program without extensive faculty involvement. There is no ideal general education model that is suitable for all community colleges, and it is very unlikely that any new general education model will be successful if the faculty members do not understand its purpose and its potential benefit for students.

At Miami–Dade, faculty members had a substantial role in identifying the general education goals, in devising a new general education model, in recommending needed academic support services, in providing creative ideas for improving students' success in general education courses, and in developing new core courses and instructional resources. The various general education committees, with a balance of administrators and faculty members, spent three years completing the general education study and recommending a new general education model. After the new general education program was approved, other faculty committees spent four years in the implementation of different parts of the general education program.

To some critics, the amount of time spent on this project may seem excessive. It may be possible for community colleges now to complete a general education revision in much less time, since more suggestions for the review process and new general education models are now available. Nevertheless, the process itself is important. Administrators and faculty need adequate time to consider general education theory, to discuss the many issues involved, to reduce excessive departmental allegiances, and to achieve consensus about a general education program that will benefit the institution as a whole, not just particular departments and faculty members.

Decision Making. In order to eliminate unnecessary conflict, one must make the process for making decisions about changes in the general education program clear at the beginning of the review. Unlike most universities, community college curriculum decisions are not always made by means of a faculty referendum. Many community colleges have representative curriculum committees that recommend substantive changes to the president or to the board of trustees.

The problem inherent in a faculty referendum on a proposed general education program is that the vote is often an all-or-nothing proposition. Faculty members naturally are most concerned with that part of the proposal that affects their courses or departments most directly. In a comprehensive proposal, there are many different parts, and no proposal can be entirely satisfactory to any one faculty member. Thus, anyone can find some aspect of the program with which to disagree and, consequently, will reject the entire proposal. If a referendum is necessary or desirable, it would seem more appropriate to vote separately on different parts of the proposal, so that rejection of one part is not necessarily a rejection of the whole. This is especially true since there are undoubtedly some administrators and faculty members who will not take the time, for whatever reasons, to examine the comprehensive proposal carefully.

At Miami–Dade, the college's existing decision-making process for curriculum changes was followed. After all faculty members had had an opportunity to make recommendations to the collegewide steering committee, a comprehensive proposal was developed and distributed for general review on two occasions. The final revision was then formally proposed to the college curriculum committee. After extensive discussion of the components, a formal vote was held for each major component of the proposal. Although some changes were made in several of the components, the basic general education model was approved by a wide margin. The amended proposal was then sent to the president's council, a body composed of the chief district and campus administrators and the campus senate presidents. The council also voted separately on each major section, and again several changes were made. The final proposal was then approved by the president and ratified by the board of trustees. The two key procedures were to allow ample time for discussion and understanding of the proposal by the decision-making groups and to vote on sections of the proposal independently.

The final decision on the basic general education model and the new general education requirements, then, was the president's. A principle was adopted early in the general education study, however, that gave responsibility for the development of the new general education core courses and the course objectives to those who would implement the general education core, the faculty. This principle was adhered to rigidly during the implementation process. Neither the president nor any other administrator ever tried to dictate the content of the new courses or the instructional methods. This clear delineation of responsibility — administrative responsibility for approving the total general education model and faculty responsibility for course development — provided a clear, appropriate decision-making process.

Review Process. Miami–Dade had success with a three-step process in its general education study: collegewide steering committee review, campus-based faculty reviews, and college standing committee reviews. This process included in-depth study of general education issues by a selected group of administrators and faculty, broad review by faculty at large, and deliberations by existing committees and councils that were part of the decision-making process.

The general education steering committee was composed of thirteen administrators and faculty, chaired by the executive vice-president. There was an even balance of administrators and faculty members. The members represented each major academic area of the college, including continuing education and student support services. While the steering committee members were very interested in the general education area, they were not necessarily expert initially in general education theory and practice. A college might have some concern that a steering committee whose members represented possibly conflicting areas would be prone to defend those interests at the expense of a balanced general education program. This did not occur with the Miami–Dade steering committee. Given adequate time for discussion and the initial focus on a rationale for general education and general education goals, the members of the steering committee clearly were more concerned with the total general education program. In fact, during the discussions in steering committee meetings, members could not be identified with the areas they represented, based on the views they expressed.

The tasks of the steering committee included meeting with departments and other faculty groups to understand their views and concerns about general education; addressing general education issues; drafting the rationale, definition, and goals of general education; reading literature in the general education area; and discussing issues and proposals with consultants who were nationally recognized experts in various general education areas. The final, most important task of the steering committee was to develop a general education model for adoption by the college. Whenever the committee drafted models or proposals, they distributed them at least twice daily to all the faculty for review and criticism. The steering committee's intent in these drafts was not simply to combine all recommended features or to act as a compromise body, but to develop, with the invaluable help of the college faculty, the very best model it could for Miami–Dade's current students and students in the decades ahead, given the needs of the Dade County community and the strengths of the Miami–Dade faculty.

After the steering committee had drafted the general education rationale, definition, and goals and had revised these several times based upon faculty comments, processes were established on each of the four campuses to have faculty recommend the best way to achieve those goals. Each campus established its own structure, ranging from a campus steering committee that was to gather suggestions from the rest of the campus faculty, to one campus's inclusion of every campus faculty member on one of nine subcommittees of approximately thirty-five faculty members each. Although the latter process may at first seem unmanageable, it does have the distinct advantage of including all faculty members directly in the general education revision. In fact, the campus that used this approach did develop sound recommendations for the collegewide steering committee.

The steering committee's final proposal for a new general education model was submitted to the collegewide curriculum committee for its action. In fact, the steering committee had been authorized originally by the collegewide curriculum committee, and the director of the general education study regularly reported the steering committee's progress to the curriculum committee. This ensured that the curriculum committee had ample opportunity to understand the reasons for the model that was finally proposed. The collegewide curriculum committee, with representation from every division on each campus, did approach the proposal as a total program and was not swayed by arguments or courses that did not correspond with the program's rationale or did not address the general education goals.

After the curriculum committee approved the plan, with some minor modifications, the proposal was forwarded to the president's council for final action. The district vice-presidents, the campus vice-presidents, and the faculty senate presidents again considered the proposal in terms of its overall ramifications and implications for future directions of the college. The council approved the new general education program in substance and made its recommendation for adoption to the president.

The council's recommendations concluded a comprehensive review process that included all faculty members, elected representatives of all departments, and administrators. Although there were still many faculty members and administrators who objected strongly to various components of the model and who had concerns about its implementation, the program had received overwhelming support throughout the formal review process.

The General Education Program

Many students who have basic skill deficiencies, poor study skills, weak academic backgrounds, and unclear educational goals enroll in community colleges. Some of these students have not had academic success in the past. Other older students return to college after years away from formal education. Many students hold part-time and even full-time jobs, have family responsibilities, and other interests in their social lives. They do not have the advantages of resident college students, who generally have the opportunity to devote more time to study and to receive special help more easily. Thus, it is imperative that community colleges develop academic support programs that will provide students with more academic assistance, better academic advisement and counseling, and close monitoring of their academic progress. Miami–Dade found that for students to achieve its general education goals, more than a system of course requirements was needed. A comprehensive approach is essential.

Developmental Programs. Most colleges do not include remedial or developmental courses as part of their general education programs. Contrary to what some instructors assert, general education is far more than the basic communications and computational skills. Nevertheless, the evidence of students' deficiencies in basic skills is overwhelming. To develop a general education model that does not provide for improvement of students' basic skills is to ignore reality.

Many community colleges have good or even excellent developmental programs. There are, however, varied assumptions underlying these programs. After many years' experience with different models for remediation, Miami–Dade in its general education study adopted several collegewide positions. First, the basic skills are so critical that remedial or developmental work cannot be optional — students must be required to demonstrate these basic competencies. Colleges should have data, usually through a testing program, with which to make decisions about students' need for developmental work. Miami–Dade now requires all students to be tested in reading, writing, and math prior to full-time students' first registration and by the seventh credit for part-time students.

There should also be clear exit competencies established for all students who complete remedial or developmental work. In the Miami–Dade program, the exit competencies in reading and writing are the entrance requirements for the core communications course. Furthermore, students who have extreme deficiencies in the basic communications skills, so that they are not prepared to take any regular college courses requiring reading and writing, need intensive programs. It is highly unlikely that a student with such serious deficiencies will be able to attain the required competencies in a three-credit course during one term, or even two, three, or four terms. These students need to devote as many hours as possible to skills development if they are realistically to have any chance to complete a degree program.

A final, most important position taken by Miami–Dade is that the development of these skills, especially the communications skills, cannot be the responsibility of one program, one group of instructors, or one course alone. Students will not become proficient in writing if they discover that they only need to demonstrate these skills in English courses. Likewise, they need to develop different kinds of critical reading skills appropriate for courses in the various curriculum areas. Miami–Dade is now in the process of developing reading, writing, and math "across the curriculum" programs. In fact, as part of its general education program, the college adopted the following principle (Lukenbill and McCabe, 1978):

> All faculty share the responsibility for assisting students in improving their reading and writing skills by giving assignments when appropriate, by reinforcing the importance of these skills, by pointing out deficiencies, and by directing students to faculty who can provide the assistance needed [p. 49].

Student Flow Model. Fundamental to the design of Miami–Dade's new general education program is its incorporation into a structured student flow model. A student flow model is important for both the college and its students. The college needs a structure that ensures that students move systematically from their first enrollment to the degrees they seek. This structure does not have to be a lock-step approach that does not allow for individual differences among students and flexibility in curricular programs. Nevertheless, the college should be in a position to assess students' progress at regular intervals and to prescribe special assistance when their progress is unsatisfactory.

Students also want and need a clear structure for completing their programs and degrees. Although they should have some opportunity to choose electives of personal interest to them and to investigate different degree programs, a degree composed of only unrelated, introductory courses, without some depth in a particular academic area, is unacceptable. This is not to say that students should be encouraged to specialize in their first college term. A strong general education program should discourage such early specialization. Contrary to what was often found in the 1960s, students today want the guidance and direction of their instructors and the college. Miami–Dade's student flow model, then, enables the college to monitor student performance and progress toward a degree, while at the same time giving students clearer direction about course sequences.

The central part of Miami–Dade's general education program is the general education core — five courses ("Communications," "Humanities," "The Individual," "The Social Environment," and "The Natural Environment") required for all degree-seeking students. These core courses were developed specifically to address the general education goals. Since enrollments in these courses will be very large, the college can justify providing substantial resources in order to assist faculty members to individualize instruction to meet the wide range of student needs.

Since the core courses are interdisciplinary, stressing basic principles, theories, developments, and learning in the broad content areas, many faculty members did not feel adequately prepared to teach the courses. As part of the commitment to provide faculty development activities, the college formed faculty development seminars. Faculty members were released from one teaching assignment for a major term in order to participate in these seminars, which had two main objectives: to prepare faculty members to teach the core courses and to develop faculty resource notebooks that could be distributed to all faculty who would teach the courses. The faculty members were able to draw from their own experiences to recommend teaching strategies, audiovisual materials, assessment procedures, and special support for students with basic skill deficiencies or physical handicaps. The resource notebooks are particularly valuable for part-time instructors.

Students in associate in arts degree programs must also complete distribution requirements. These fifteen credits must be taken in the areas of English composition, mathematics, the humanities, the social sciences, and the natural sciences. The students, however, do not have unlimited choices for meeting the distribution requirements. The six to eight courses in each distribution group have to meet specific criteria to qualify for inclusion in the group. A distribution course must address general educational goals, emphasize values, broad principles, and problem solving, illustrate relationships with other disciplines in the areas, and must not be designed exclusively as a preparation for a major area of study or for a particular career. Students cannot take a distribution course until they have completed the core course in that area.

In addition to the fifteen-credit core and the fifteen credits of distribution courses, students must complete six credits from a relatively large list of general education elective courses. This progression from core courses to distribution courses to general education electives to special program courses enables the college to assess students' progress at each stage. The college wants to be certain that by the time the students have completed the core courses, they have acquired those communications skills that are essential for success in the more in-depth discipline courses. Other collegewide assessments, apart from regular course exams, may be given after the distribution level and again prior to graduation.

Academic Support Services. To provide academic support for students as they progress through the general education courses and their particular occupational or transfer programs, Miami–Dade has developed several support systems. These systems are critical for enabling the college to identify students with academic difficulty soon enough to provide the needed help.

The first system to be adopted was a new set of academic standards. The rationale for rigorous standards applied to students early in their academic careers is not to penalize students but rather to provide them with assistance early enough to do them some good. As early as after the first seven credits, a student may fall in the "academic warning" category. This category and subsequent categories require students to reduce their course loads and to take developmental courses, counseling, or other courses prescribed by the college.

The final category, before dismissal, is suspension. Students suspended for a major term may return only in a probationary status and must maintain a C average. Over a three-year period, Miami–Dade suspended approximately 11,000 students. The college's intent is not to deprive these students of the opportunity to pursue a college education; nevertheless, the college believes that students must demonstrate that they can make profitable use of the college's resources. The college cannot justify expending public funds for students who are not making reasonable progress in their programs. A number of these 11,000 students did return to the college and are now being successful. The others who did not return would probably not have completed their programs anyway and would have withdrawn from the college.

Two other systems, Academic Alert and the Advisement and Graduation Information System (AGIS), provide much more complete advisement information to both students and instructors. By means of computer programs, all credit students are "alerted" midway through each term about their progress. Information from the student data file, from basic skills test results, and from instructors' reports on students' progress and attendance at classes is used to generate individualized letters that advise students about specific steps they should take if they are having difficulty. Research indicates that the majority of those students who are warned about their lack of progress do complete their courses satisfactorily.

The AGIS program provides such comprehensive information about students' educational goals, the courses they have completed, and the courses needed to achieve their goals, that a faculty member can advise almost any student about what courses to take. Instructors can know at a glance what general education requirements the student has completed and for which courses the student is currently enrolled or enrolled for a future term. A special feature of the program provides specific transfer information for all Florida universities and local colleges. This document, in effect, is a three-way contract among the student, Miami–Dade, and the four-year college or university that specifies what courses the student must complete in order to transfer as a junior without having to take additional lower-divison courses. It is the AGIS program, together with the academic standards and the Academic Alert System, that enables Miami–Dade to monitor student progress and to provide the special assistance needed for students to complete their general education program and their other degree requirements.

Conclusion

What, then, should be the role of the new American community college? Most importantly, it must maintain its essential commitment to the open door, as it now stands as the pivotal institution in salvaging opportunity for the large number of Americans whose academic and occupational skills have not prepared them to participate in society or to achieve any measure of success. There could be no more vital or challenging responsibility. At the same time, the community college must place emphasis on achievement and hold to high expectations for program completion — in other words, the goal is excellence for everyone. Ultimately, no one benefits when individuals simply pass through the program and become certified while lacking the competencies indicated by those certifications.

Dealing with the dilemma of lower skills of entering students and higher expectations for completion will be very different and, in many cases, will call for widespread reform of general education programs. Institutions must address these problems with a dedicated spirit toward a new direction and with full understanding of the great importance of their work. Community colleges need to implement programs that:

- Raise expectations for effort and performance from students
- Provide students more direction and fewer options as they progress through the college program
- Provide students more feedback regarding progress, and early and continued information on performance problems
- Provide increased personal and instructional support to those experiencing difficulty
- Place a focus on academic achievement and performance, including expanded opportunities for superior and talented students

- Clearly set a point at which a student's performance must demonstrate academic progress in order to remain in the college.

Throughout the country, there is evidence that action in these new directions is already developing.

Reference

Lukenbill, J. D., and McCabe, R. H. *General Education in a Changing Society.* Dubuque, Iowa: Kendall/Hunt, 1978.

Jeffrey D. Lukenbill is director of the General Education Project at Miami–Dade Community College.

Robert H. McCabe is president of Miami–Dade Community College.

Transfer-oriented general education is now at a crossroads.

General Education and the Transfer Function

Leslie Koltai

The plight of transfer-oriented general education in American community colleges has reached disaster proportions. Dramatic declines in enrollment, student performance and persistence, faculty commitment, and institutional coordination clearly indicate that the problem demands urgent attention.

This situation is at least partially the result of a national educational philosophy that, during the past two decades, has evolved away from emphasis on skills, competencies, and proficiencies and toward self-directed instruction that was supposed to be either "fun" or "relevant" in terms of career preparation. We now have classrooms filled with unpracticed learners whose elementary and secondary school experiences have encouraged them to think that they are supposed to be entertained by their instructors, with little or no effort or commitment required on their part. On the other hand, we have faculty who resist making written assignments and continually opt for multiple choice or true/false tests rather than the more difficult to grade but usually more challenging essay exams. In short, today's general education transfer offerings seldom encourage critical or even independent thought. Students find them to be without rigor and, consequently, without reward.

B. L. Johnson, (Ed.). *New Directions for Community Colleges: General Education in Two-Year Colleges*, no. 40. San Francisco: Jossey-Bass, December 1982.

According to Cohen and Brawer (1982) in their recent book, *The American Community College,* general education in two-year institutions has also fallen prey to "faculty power, lack of student interest, increased demands on faculty time, difficulty in integrating disciplines, and, most of all, from its lack of demonstrated value and the superficiality of the presentations."

Also causing general education's decline have been increased course/unit commitments demanded by career-oriented programs. We have seen an overemphasis on "preprofessional" studies, with students neglecting general education in favor of course work related to their chosen profession, and this has been accompanied by greater emphasis on faculty specialization.

Symptomatic of the problem are loss of proprietorship among faculty and counselors, a generally lethargic approach to curricular revitalization, widely divergent articulation agreements, and the absence of structured, sequential, degree-related course configurations. In fact, Astin (1977) observes that, for freshmen aspiring to earn a baccalaureate degree, chances of attaining that goal are diminished if they begin their studies at a community college. In California, the number of community college students transferring each year to the University of California and California State University systems increased from 48,700 in 1969–1970 to 60,700 in 1975–1976, then declined to 51,900 by 1979–1980. This represents a 14.5 percent decline from 1969 to 1979. In other words, more and more of our students are not succeeding in their transfer goals.

There are those, however, who ask how we can possibly solve the problem of general transfer education when we educators cannot even seem to agree upon a definition of this field of study. For the purpose of this discussion, it suffices to say that general education encompasses, but is not limited to, the generic skills of clear and critical thought, coherent written and spoken expression, and the ability to deal effectively with quantitative issues. General education is not a collection of facts—it is a point of view with application in all areas of study. It is a safety net of knowledge beneath us as we attempt to live and work effectively on the tightrope of modern life.

When our students transfer to four-year institutions, their general education background should signify a certain level of competency, an ability to reach beyond a recital of facts in order to recognize and deal with the implications beyond those facts. General education, then, can bring far more than just the traditional rewards of learning. It can mean an awakening, an intellectual lifestyle that offers a broader range of choice.

In California, the real thrust to strengthen general education came about as a result of a mandate from the University of California, when that system began to require four years of high school English for admission. And the thrust became stronger in 1980 when the California State University system called for more rigorous general education requirements for admission. Since the state university systems were becoming more stringent — and since community colleges supply 60 percent of the universities' entering junior classes — it was clear that two-year institutions must carry the general education ball.

In California's community colleges, efforts are already underway to revitalize the general education transfer function through strengthening requirements in English composition, math competency, and critical thinking. The California Community College board of governors voted recently to implement a more structured general education package that is still flexible enough to meet the varying articulation requirements of four-year institutions.

Efforts to revitalize the general education transfer function must involve more than just community colleges, however. These efforts must involve actively the external community, including the public at large, four-year institutions, and secondary schools, as well as the internal community composed of students, faculty, counselors, and administrators.

The External Factors

General Public. In terms of the broadest segment of the external community (the public at large), our efforts must be devoted to demonstrating the value of general education for all students, whether transfer-oriented or not. As educators, however, we have failed thus far to persuade the tax-paying public that the benefits of a general education background are personal, professional, and economic — that pursuing this course of study is, in effect, a form of down payment on the future.

The general public must be convinced that an employable person in today's job market is one who possesses broad general knowledge in sciences and the arts, in addition to skills in reading, writing, speaking, and math. In fact, the qualification for basic literacy will soon include computer skills as well.

Four-Year Institutions. The second set of external factors are those involving four-year institutions. To be successful, community college transfer programs require development of a new partnership with four-year institutions — a partnership that will benefit both educational sectors (as well as the students we all seek to serve) as we develop and implement a strong mutual commitment to general education. The key to this improved relationship in higher education is the establishment of more effective communication between its components. There are several specific areas that are of prime mutual concern; these include student performance and preparedness, remediation, articulation and certification, basic skills, and student needs.

Student Performance and Preparedness. Crucial to the first of these concerns is the matter of evaluation of student performance at the university level. Frankly, we need the university's assistance in determining how transfer students do when they reach the four-year institutions. Unfortunately, there is little published information of a specific nature on transfer student performance. Thus, we are left without a valuable tool for effective evaluation of programs, classes, and even instructors.

There are some reports that tell, in summary fashion, of the cumulative grade point average, but those reports seldom provide detailed infromation. We need information that links the performance of our graduates with specific study areas. Without these data, it is difficult at best to evaluate the job we are doing in preparing students for four-year classrooms.

If, on the other hand, we were to determine that our transfer students were not doing well in math, for example, or in English composition, then we could take a hard look at the classes we offered them, the instructors they studied under, and so on. We could take concrete, specific action to ensure that future transfer students performed at a more acceptable level.

Remediation. Traditionally, this function has been designated as a responsibility of the community college. However, one cannot help but note the number of university courses being offered for credit that fall into this category, while many of those same courses at community colleges are not accepted for credit by four-year institutions.

One of the benefits of improved communication between community colleges and four-year institutions is that we would be able to let our students know exactly what courses to take at our institutions in order to be prepared to transfer. This improved dialogue would permit us to determine more accurately the level of proficiency our students will be expected to demonstrate, and it will also assist us in directing students in the proper course of lower-division study.

Articulation and Certification. The major complication in this area is the fact that classes that meet the general education criteria at one campus of a multicampus university are not necessarily deemed acceptable at another. Here is yet another reason for improving cooperation between the community college and the four-year institution.

Student Needs. Community colleges can contribute to a more effective partnership with four-year institutions by providing them with a wealth of information about exactly who our graduates are and what they are looking for in a transfer institution. For example, the Los Angeles Community College District's (LACCD) research division has shown that approximately 80 percent of our students work full- or part-time while attending college. Only one out of four students is enrolled full-time. The rest fit their class schedules around working hours or other outside commitments, which means that evening classes are often their only alternative. In fact, more than 40 percent of LACCD students attend evening classes. These statistics are not atypical for community colleges nationwide, particularly in urban areas. And yet many four-year institutions do not make evening classes accessible for students who can realistically find no other path to a bachelor's degree.

It is an important role of community colleges to identify and prepare potential transfers for four-year colleges and universities. We have a legitimate right to ask what those institutions plan to do to increase the transferring student's expectations of success. The possibilities are deceptively simple. For example, we suggest that transferring students be provided with at least the same quality of orientation that native freshman receive. Also beneficial are campus tours and assistance with filing applications.

High Schools. Efforts to revitalize general education at the community college and university level will accomplish little, however, unless they are tied to cooperative efforts in high schools.

According to Ernest Boyer ("A Conversation... , 1982), president of The Carnegie Foundation for the Advancement of Teaching, "both the colleges and the high schools have an obligation to develop a program of general education that makes sense," adding that "much of the curriculum confusion in high school has occurred because higher education has seemed so confused over the definition of an educated person" (p. 19). When four-year colleges and universities relaxed the course requirements for admissions, they paved the way for less stringent high school graduation requirements.

Maeroff (1982) points out that even "the highly publicized core curriculum at Harvard College, developed over a period of five and a half years, might as well have been fashioned in a vacuum so far as the secondary schools were concerned," since Harvard "never bothered asking" superintendents or principals of principal feeder high schools "what they thought of the proposed changes and how their curriculums would be affected."

Yes, better communication and cooperation are urgently needed. And the "daisy chain" of cooperation offers unlimited possibilities. Students from four-year institutions could tutor their community college counterparts, providing needed individual attention as well as a personal link for the potential transfer student. Community college enrollees could provide similar services for local high school students, thus enhancing their own understanding of general education material.

In addition, community college students could be invited to attend classes, lectures, and seminars on the four-year campus while, at the same time, high school students could be offered access to the community college classrooms, libraries, and activity rooms. Costly and rapidly obsolete equipment could be shared among all three sectors, providing students with exposure to more educational resources than any single institution would be able to provide alone.

Another idea worth investigating is encouraging faculty from the four-year institutions to offer guest lectures at community colleges, while faculty from the latter institutions could make their lecturing services available to high school classes. This could provide an excellent opportunity for faculty revitalization, as well as offering students at each level of feeder institution exposure to the materials and instruction that they will encounter after matriculation. Also suggested is an informal "adoption" of particular high schools by local community or four-year colleges.

At the Los Angeles Community College District, we have been working extensively with local feeder high schools in order to coordinate activities designed to improve communication between potential transfer students, secondary school instructors, and LACCD faculty. Among the activities discussed or already conducted are regionalized campus tours, issuance of library cards for our facilities, and informational sessions at the high schools. In addition, we have developed a half-hour telephone/television video network presentation during which counselors from high schools, community colleges, and the University of California, Los Angeles, are available to answer viewers' questions about college entrance and transfer. Efforts are now under way to expand this presentation to an hour. We are also discussing development of videotape "tours" of our campuses that would be made available to local high schools for use with twelfth graders.

Internal Revitalization

Jerry G. Gaff (1980), director of the Project of General Education Models, wrote that one of the more curious aspects of general education reform is the fact that debate usually concerns curricular philosophy, structures, and subject matter — with "little attention given to students."

Such reform, he continues, is often undertaken "without the meaningful involvement of students, and the discussions seldom reflect a sensitive and detailed understanding of students as persons and as learners."

Partly because of this omission, the knowledge that students do possess is often fragmented, with little or no awareness of, or experience in, connecting those fragments. Students often don't see the connections among the various disciplines they are studying, let alone between their coursework and their life off-campus. They need their instructors and their counselors to show them how to make that connection.

Students are also taking fewer and fewer courses each semester, which means that they are having less and less contact with faculty, with counselors, and with advisors. Since many of our students represent the first generation of their families to attend college, they aren't familiar with how to survive on campus or with how to avail themselves of the support services needed for their collegiate success. They simply do not know what to expect or how to cope in a college environment.

In addition, many of our faculty have gotten out of the habit of interacting with students. Some counselors have forfeited their role of directing students to the classes in which they have a realistic expectation of success. They permit students to pick and choose courses with little or no intervention or guidance. And when these poorly prepared students reach the classroom, they are often confounded by a system that places developmental instruction on the lowest rungs of its priority ladder.

Medsker and Tillery (1971), in their book *Breaking the Access Barriers,* wrote that some instructors are more interested in academic rank, tenure, and teacher rights than in actual instruction. The authors say that these instructors are concerned with "status," and do not feel that teaching developmental or remedial courses identifies them with academia. Medsker and Tillery compare this attitude to the doctor who refuses to take "hard-to-cure" cases, and they accuse those instructors of contributing to what is developing into a "ridiculously high attrition rate."

To help combat this problem, the California State University (CSU) system and the Los Angeles Community College District have established a cooperative project, the Faculty Institute for the Improvement of Basic Skills Instruction, to offer a positive approach to dealing with declining student basic skills. The primary goal of the institute is to work with faculty members who are teaching basic skills, as well as with instructors in other disciplines who can reinforce those efforts.

The program is being carried out in part through a cluster system in which a CSU campus is teamed with the three community colleges that contribute the majority of that university's upper-division students. Intersystem committees in writing, reading, mathematics, and English as a second language are responding to current developments in each of those fields. In this way, it is hoped that cooperative work on shared problems will lead to new teaching strategies to accommodate today's students.

In addition, the LACCD's Developmental Skills Project is providing additional funds for learning centers and developmental skills instructors to give special assistance in basic skills. And our Computer-Assisted Instruction Developmental Project is designed to determine the instructional impact of such technologies as computer-managed instruction, computer-based instruction, and the related use of media.

Other instructional strategies include the Improvement of Learning in English Project, which is designed to help faculty become more effective in English instruction. This project provides paraprofessional assistants in English classes that use the one-to-one method of teaching composition. It is estimated that more than 5,000 LACCD students benefitted from personalized instruction during 1980–1981.

Key to assisting transfer students in reaching their personal, academic, and professional goals, however, is the use of valid assessment tools by which to evaluate previously acquired skills. Assessment tools are needed for guidance, counseling, and direction into courses and fields of study in which the student has a reasonable expectation of success.

A valid assessment tool can result in more effective use of the student's abilities, as well as in more efficient utilization of institutional resources — including faculty time and effort. In this way, students may begin college by taking courses in which they have a reasonable expectation of success. All students demonstrating a need for remediation in basic skills should be required to enroll in and complete the appropriate developmental courses before enrolling in regular courses requiring those skills.

Also needed are means by which to serve superior students, who have been somewhat overlooked in institutional preoccupation with serving their less-prepared classmates. Special honors courses, high-intensity minicourses with interdisciplinary orientation, and classes at neighboring four-year institutions are all options to be explored.

Of course, earlier identification of potential transfer students is imperative if these types of support activities are to be successful. Such identification should be coupled with exposure to counselors who are knowledgeable about transfer requirements.

The Los Angeles Community College District has recently

begun contacting all students with a 2.5 grade point average in forty-five units or more, notifying them of their transfer options and offering them assistance in evaluating their opportunities for continued education. This same list has been supplied to local campuses of the University of California and CSU systems, which have, in turn, sent letters inviting those students to investigate continuing their educational experiences. Future mailings will be done for students with thirty units or more maintaining a 2.0 grade point average.

Also beneficial is establishment of "transfer clubs," with each group tied to a different four-year institution. These clubs can function as support groups for potential transfers, providing them with companionship, assistance, and shared goals.

Worthwhile, too, are activities such as Educational Opportunity Program (EOP) conferences, financial aid workshops for transfers, career seminars, videotapes on senior institutions, peer advising (by those who have transferred), specially prepared packets, field trips, transfer newsletters, catalogues on microfiche, and other informational materials. Such activities could be organized and administered effectively by a transfer information center, which could also assume responsibility for developing articulation agreements, arranging workshops between counselors and representatives of local universities, and developing computerized and printed information for counselors and faculty.

Transfer-oriented general education is now at a crossroads. It can move with strength and vigor to a redefined, highly valued place on this country's educational landscape, or it can stumble weakly toward a tragic demise. The next few years will make the difference.

References

Astin, A. W. *Four Critical Years*. San Francisco: Jossey-Bass, 1977.

"A Conversation with Ernest Boyer." *Change*, 1982, *14* (1), 18–21.

Cohen, A. M., and Brawer, F. B. *The American Community College*. San Francisco: Jossey-Bass, 1982.

Gaff, J. G. "Objectives for Students." In J. G. Gaff and others (Eds.), *General Education: Issues and Resources*. Washington, D.C.: Association of American Colleges; and New Haven, Conn.: Society for Values in Higher Education, 1980.

Maeroff, G. I. "Ties That Do Not Bind," *Change*, 1982, *14* (1), 12–17, 46–51.

Medsker, L. L., and Tillery, D. S. *Breaking the Access Barrier. A Profile of Two-Year Colleges*. New York: McGraw-Hill, 1971.

Leslie Koltai is chancellor, Los Angeles Community College District.

Material abstracted from recent additions to the ERIC
database provides further information on general education.

Sources and Information

James C. Palmer

The preceding chapters examine a wide range of topics related to general education at two-year colleges. As a bibliographic aid to readers interested in obtaining additional information, this concluding chapter cites ERIC documents and journal articles that deal with general education planning and programming. The following paragraphs will review these documents and articles under five headings: the general education agenda; curriculum and course development; general education in vocational programs; guidelines and models; and practices.

The General Education Agenda

Several authors present definitions of general education, revealing a wide spectrum of pedagogical objectives. These objectives "range from acquisition of survival or coping skills to the realization of one's potential as. . . [an] individual" (Tighe, 1977, p. 13). These varied objectives, however, center around a common theme: the development of the student as a person, rather than the communication of traditional academic knowledge.

Marsee (1979 and 1980) argues that general education, in the tradition of liberal studies, should help people live with themselves, develop wisdom and character, mature psychologically, and continue a

B. L. Johnson, (Ed.). *New Directions for Community Colleges: General Education in Two-Year Colleges*, no. 40.
San Francisco: Jossey-Bass, December 1982.

program of lifelong learning. He calls for general education courses that pertain directly to the lives of students, that encourage them to take responsibility for their own learning, and that provide them with an understanding of what scholarly work entails.

The complexity of modern society, however, has prompted other authors to stress coping skills as a prerequisite to this personal and intellectual development. Moore (1978) argues that it is no longer adequate to help the individual become economically self-sufficient and socially responsible. "The student," he maintains, "must also learn how to cope with technology, protect him or herself against exploitation, and confront and handle conflict in a culture of ambiguity" (p. 14). Likewise, Quistwater (1979) maintains that college resources should be reallocated to provide general education courses in the areas of future studies, cope-ability development, and other topics related to the personal and career survival of those born at the end of the postwar baby boom and in the mid and late 1960s.

While the community college is often referred to as an ideal setting at which to carry out this broad, multidisciplinary agenda, some authors warn of the barriers to general education that are inherent in the traditional administrative organizations of the colleges and in their growing commitment to vocationalism. Duffey (1981) writes that the growing demands for general education are a reflection of the populist heritage of the community college. Preusser (1978), on the other hand, notes that, rather than putting their full innovative energy and interest into meeting the demands of general education students, community colleges have been too concerned with establishing an identity within higher education and have thus structured departments based on existing systems at four-year colleges.

Cohen (1978) cites other impediments, including the failure of educators to develop a consistent definition of general education, a lack of leadership in the field, and the overall decline in literacy. As another example, Sanborn (1979) argues that community colleges have developed a market-oriented, vocational mission at the expense of general education. As a result, Sanborn warns, the "new students" of the 1970s have been shunted into terminal career curricula and have thus been denied access to education.

Curriculum and Course Development

Course and curriculum development have received a great deal of attention in the general education literature. Matthews (1979) compares the general education curricula recommended by B. Lamar Johnson in

General Education in Action (1952) with the curriculum developed in the late 1970s at Miami-Dade Community College (Florida). Among other findings, Matthews notes that while technology, value systems, personal social development, career goals, and national culture were common general education themes in the 1950s, issues related to energy, discretionary time, and lifelong learning have since gained importance.

The question of curriculum design is broached by Hammons and others (1980) and by Henderson and Henderson (1978). Hammons and others review the findings of a survey of a random sample of 254 public two-year colleges. The authors found that, for all the general education curricula areas investigated (that is, communications, art and humanities, mathematics, natural sciences, health, and social sciences), the most common curricular approach consisted of a distribution of single-discipline, subject-centered courses. Curricular approaches utilized less frequently included single courses based on topics, issues, and problems; multidisciplinary courses; and the "infusion" approach, which rather than providing a core of specific courses, links all college activities with general education objectives.

Henderson and Henderson (1978) present a historical review of the various curricular approaches that have been utilized in general education, including the distribution plan, survey courses, the block-and-gap curriculum, and the development of courses that are oriented to broad cultural interests rather than to professional or vocational preparation. While these approaches, the authors argue, provide intellectual breadth, they do not necessarily foster intellectual and personal growth. General education courses, the Hendersons conclude, should present subject matter that not only promotes intellectual breadth but that also sufficiently motivates the student to take those actions necessary for him or her to secure "an improved way of life" (p. 23).

Central to the problem of curriculum design is the development of instructional delivery systems that address the varying interests and needs of transfer students, vocational students, and students who are attending for personal enrichment. Miller (1978) argues that general education instructors should try a variety of instructional approaches, rather than repeatedly using a method that appeals to only one group and that stresses one cognitive style. Marks (1975) urges the development of a two-pronged curriculum with courses that meet the university-oriented needs of transfer students as well as courses for students seeking cultural enrichment. The synthesis of a common core curriculum is addressed by Richter (1978), who presents recommendations for the development of natural sciences courses that encompass both scientific and social issues. Such courses, Richter argues, should include a cross section of the college's diverse student population, stress the development of scientific literacy, present the world as a set of interdependent subsystems, and utilize the entire community as a learning environment.

General Education in Vocational Programs

Still another curricular concern is the role and delivery of general education in college vocational programs.

Bartkovich (1981) delineates arguments both for and against the inclusion of general education in vocational curricula. Arguments for general education, he notes, are based on humanistic, pragmatic, and theoretical orientations. Arguments for the limitation or exclusion of general education focus on students' desires for additional technical courses, the unnecessary lengthening of vocational programs by general education requirements, and the belief that students' personal and social growth can be achieved without general education.

Clavner and Sumodi (1981) detail the importance of general education in the area of allied health technology. Noting the interpersonal skills needed by health care professionals to understand patient needs and survive in the complex environment of a hospital, the authors argue that colleges have an obligation to incorporate general education in health technology curricula.

In relation to the delivery of general education, Brawley (1980) urges educators to provide general education courses only after the student has completed in-depth vocational studies. Arguing that this is the most effective approach, he details its application in a human services curriculum and enumerates the vocational and general education competencies to be achieved by students.

Finally, Morgan (1978) examines the administration of general education programs in two-year vocational/technical institutes. Noting the fact that conflict between general education instructors and vocational teachers places general education staff on the defensive, Morgan argues that (1) general education be considered in the curriculum planning process; (2) general education instructors work together with vocational staff in developing instructional materials so as to increase communication; (3) general education instructors find additional ways of making their courses relevant to students; and (4) employers should be reminded that general education produces well-rounded workers.

Curriculum Guidelines and Models

Included in the literature are suggested guidelines and curricular models that can be used by educators who are faced with the task of developing a general education program.

Shaw (1981), drawing from experiences with general education at the Dallas County Community College District, outlines five principles of program development: (1) each college must develop its own goals for general education; (2) staff must be allowed time to become familiar with and committed to these goals; (3) the goals must have community affirmation; (4) faculty commitment to general education is essential; and (5) the goals must be incorporated into the institutional planning process. Shaw also warns against adopting university models for general education that are unsuited to today's nontraditional student.

Piland (1981) urges curriculum planners to establish first a general education task force comprised of faculty, administrators, and students from traditional general education program areas, as well as from the college's vocational areas. The task force is designed to identify specific goals and learning objectives for a general education program that (1) employs an interdisciplinary approach, (2) encourages team teaching, (3) promotes student involvement with the community through volunteer work and other activities, (4) provides students with career information as well as academic studies, (5) includes basic business education, (6) teaches computer literacy, and (7) includes independent study.

Strasser (1979) examines general education in light of the important roles community colleges play in providing adult continuing education. Drawing from an analysis of the general education program at Montgomery College (Maryland), Strasser discusses several guidelines regarding general education for adult students. Among other items, these guidelines call for a coherent and structured program, flexible scheduling to meet the needs of working adults, courses that allow students to apply academic knowledge to contemporary problems, the utilization of modules with varying credit length, and the establishment of appropriate distribution requirements for students working toward a degree. The author also provides suggested course titles as well as a general resource bibliography.

Finally, Cohen and Brawer (1982) argue that a "general education pattern for all community college students can be devised if the staff adheres to certain premises" (p. 334). These premises call for a faculty role in defining the general education program; the appointment of a dean, chairperson, or other administrator to head the program; and the management of the program at the campus rather than on the district level. Cohen and Brawer then outline a "utopian" general education model centered around a faculty that is organized into four divisions: culture, communications, institutions, and environment. According to the model, the general education program is to have its own budget; general education modules are to be developed for vocational courses;

and separate general education courses are to be developed for collegiate and developmental students.

Practices

Besides position papers and curriculum models, the ERIC database includes a number of documents that describe the planning, implementation, and evaluation of community college general education programs.

Halyard and Murphy (1978) describe the implementation of a competency-based general education program at Piedmont Technical College in South Carolina. The implementation process involved the identification of requisite communications and reasoning competencies through surveys of faculty, students, and area industries. The competencies generated by these activities were used to develop the educational delivery system in which students (1) "sequentially master speaking, reading, listening, and writing skills as a total interrelated process at all levels rather than as separate activities" (p. 17); and (2) develop reasoning skills in a required three-hour course devoted to career development.

Walker (1980) examines the rationale upon which Pensacola Junior College (Florida) planned, in 1980, to determine competencies, prerequisites, and course sequences for a general education program. Under this rationale, courses will progressively strengthen the student's decision-making skills by providing information on scientific, political, and cultural issues. By clearly defining the purpose of the general education program, the college hopes to document and justify its place in the curriculum.

The general education implementation project undertaken at Central YMCA Community College (Illinois) is described by Moline and others (1981). Included in the process was a general education consultant as well as a design team composed of faculty members who assembled the general education sequence. The sequence consisted of courses in choice and responsibility, distance and encounter, and portent and design. Instructional materials were then designed for the courses, instructors were recruited, and the courses were publicized.

Clowes and others (1979) describe the general education curricula at Miami-Dade Community College (Florida) and Cedar Valley College (Texas) to illustrate the outcomes of a "telic" curriculum revision based on (1) the collective identification of the purposes of general education by the faculty and (2) the design of a general education curriculum that reconciles those identified purposes with the interests and needs of nontraditional students. The Miami-Dade program consists of a core of five required courses as well as distribution requirements. The core courses "are not intended as the first step in a discipline, nor as the beginning of a major" (p. 11). The Cedar Valley program rests on a set of "Skills for Living" competencies related to the individual as a consumer and worker; and his or her creative and futuristic approaches to life. These competencies are incorporated throughout the curriculum rather than through core or interdisciplinary courses. Additional information about the Miami-Dade and Cedar Valley programs can be found, respectively, in Lukenbill and McCabe (1978) and Shaw (1981).

Cantor (1980) reviews the general education curricula at three institutions within the State University of New York (SUNY). The first, SUNY at Plattsburgh, incorporates a basic skills component, distributive course requirements, and integrative courses centering on themes or current issues. The second, SUNY at Brockport, consists of a required liberal arts course, communications and quantitative competency requirements, a breadth component, and a course on contemporary issues. The third, SUNY at Fredonia, involves distribution requirements among courses related to the natural and physical world, human expression, and human behavior and systems.

Interdisciplinary general education programs at Bloomfield College (New Jersey) and at Valencia Community College (Florida) are described in two additional ERIC documents. Sadler (1978) reviews a set of four interdisciplinary courses that are required of all day students at Bloomfield. The courses concentrate on literature, social sciences, mathematics, and natural sciences. Teachers representing a variety of disciplines work together in these courses to emphasize that they require common skills, such as reading and reasoning. The program at Valencia Community College is a two-year course of study that concentrates on Western intellectual history and fosters the thinking, integrating, and communications skills by which knowledge is acquired (*I.D.S.*, 1980).

Finally, Hinrichsen (1977) details the methodology and findings of a survey of 1,903 students who had enrolled in history and political science courses that were offered by Cerritos Colleges (California) as part of a required general education curriculum. Among other items, the survey instrument asked students if they would have enrolled had the courses not been required. Only 31.3 percent indicated they would have enrolled anyway; 53.4 percent would not have enrolled, and 15.3 percent had no opinion.

Conclusion

A review of the literature indicates that general education, while posing a challenge to the administrative and pedagogical skills of college staff, has been and will continue to be a cornerstone of community college education. Documents and articles cited in this review detail several problems encountered in general education programming. These include varying definitions of general education, the problem of developing instructional delivery systems for students with varied interests and objectives, and the isolation of general education staff from vocational faculty. Yet the importance of general education is underscored by almost all authors. Cohen and Brawer (1982) assert that community colleges, through general education, are responsible in the United States for furthering "the ways of knowing and the common beliefs and language that bind the society together" (p. 329). Duffey (1981), as another example, writes that community colleges are democratizing knowledge through the general education curricula that address ideals and values in addition to employable skills. And Marsee (1980) states that general education goals must be incorporated into the college mission if the community college is to remain a teaching institution. Educational writers, in short, view the implementation and promotion of the general education curriculum as being vital to both the student and to the future viability of the institution.

References

Bartkovich, J. "The General Education Component in Vocational Technical Programs Debate: From a Community College Perspective." Unpublished paper, 1981. 26 pp. (ED 208 920)

Brawley, E. A. "The Place of Liberal Education in Community College Programs for the Human Services." *Community College Review*, 1980, *7* (4), 4–10.

Cantor, H. (Ed.). *Proceedings of the SUNY Inter-Campus Conference on General Education (Utica, New York, March 26–28, 1980)*. Utica, N.Y.: Community College General Education Association, 1980. 67 pp. (ED 196 488)

Clavner, J. B., and Sumodi, V. "The Other Courses: Nurses Cannot Live on Medical Terminology Alone." Paper presented at the "Health Careers: Prescription for the 1980s" Conference, Cleveland, Ohio, March 29–April 1, 1981. 19 pp. (ED 203 926)

Clowes, D. A., Lukenbill, J. D., and Shaw, R. G. "General Education in the Community College: A Search for Purpose." Paper presented at the 59th Annual Convention of the American Association of Community and Junior Colleges, Chicago, Illinois, April 29–May 2, 1979. 25 pp. (ED 192 832)

Cohen, A. M. "The Case for General Education in Community Colleges." Paper presented at the Forum on Future Purposes, Content, and Formats for the General Education of Community College Students, Montgomery College, Maryland, May 22, 1978. 43 pp. (ED 154 849)

Cohen, A. M., and Brawer, F. B. *The American Community College*. San Francisco: Jossey-Bass, 1982. 468 pp. (ED 213 469)

Duffey, J. "Do We Still Believe We Can Shape Society?" Paper presented at the 61st Annual Convention of the American Association of Community and Junior Colleges, Washington, D.C., April 20–22, 1981. 12 pp. (ED 203 951)

Halyard, R. A., and Murphy, N. "Using Competency-Based Techniques in Curriculum Development." Papers presented at the 58th Annual Convention of the American Association of Community and Junior Colleges, Atlanta, Georgia, April 9-12, 1978. 22 pp. (ED 154 868)

Hammons, J., Thomas, W., and Ward, S. "General Education in the Community College." *Community College Frontiers,* 1980, *8* (3), 22-28.

Henderson, A. D., and Henderson J. G. "Revitalizing General Education in the Community College." Paper presented at the Forum on Future Purposes, Content, and Formats for the General Education of Community College Students, Montgomery College, Maryland, May 22, 1978. 43 pp. (ED 157 565)

Hinrichsen, K. A. "Meeting History's and Institutions' Requirements in the California Community Colleges: An Assessment of General Education and Graduation Instructional Alternatives for Cerritos College." Ed.D. dissertation, Nova University, 1977. 196 pp. (ED 148 410)

I. D. S. (Interdisciplinary Studies in General Education): A Program for the 80s. Orlando, Fla.: Valencia Community College, 1980. 9 pp. (ED 207 635)

Johnson, B. L. *General Education in Action.* Washington, D.C.: American Council on Education, 1952.

Lukenbill, J. D., and McCabe, R. H. *General Education in a Changing Society: General Education Program, Basic Skills Requirements, Standards of Academic Progress at Miami-Dade Community College.* Miami, Fla.: Office of Institutional Research, Miami-Dade Community College, 1978. 98 pp. (ED 158 812)

Marks, J. L. "Goals Conflict in Humanities Education." Unpublished paper, 1979. 13 pp. (ED 160 171)

Marsee, S. E. "General Education! Not Again?" Unpublished paper, 1979. 11 pp. (ED 164 041)

Marsee, S. E. "A President's View of the Liberal Arts." Unpublished paper, 1980. 8 pp. (ED 180 543)

Matthews, D. R., Jr. "Perspective: General Education at the Community College, 1952-1978." Graduate seminar paper, University of Florida, 1979. 23 pp. (ED 178 127)

Miller, L. W. "General Education—Dream of Coherence." Paper presented at the Forum on Future Purposes, Content, and Formats for the General Education of Community College Students, Montgomery College, Maryland, May 22, 1978. 63 pp. (ED 168 616)

Moline, L. G., Mayfield, M. K., and Embree, A. C. "STANDPOINTS: A Model for Common Learning." Paper presented at the Conference of the Association for General and Liberal Studies, Rochester, New York, November 5-7, 1981. 11 pp. (ED 210 072)

Moore, W., Jr. "The Role of General Education in the Community College." Paper presented at the Forum on Future Purposes, Content, and Formats for the General Education of Community College Students, Montgomery College, Maryland, May 22, 1978. 39 pp. (ED 167 216)

Morgan, G. M. "Why Do I Need This #*#*# Stuff for? or Importance of General Education in VTAE in Wisconsin." Unpublished paper, 1978. 17 pp. (ED 176 841)

Piland, W. E. "General Education in Community Colleges: Now and in the Future." *Community College Review,* 1981, *9* (1), 32-39.

Preusser, J. W. "General Education: Refrain or Retain." Unpublished paper, 1978. 12 pp. (ED 168 632)

Quistwater, J. M. R. "General Education for the Too-Late Generation." Paper presented to the 2nd annual assembly of the education section of the World Future Society, Minneapolis, Minn., October 19, 1979. 24 pp. (ED 180 569)

Richter, W. "General Education Natural Science for a Changing Society: Quo Vadimus?" Graduate seminar paper, University of Florida, 1978. 22 pp. (ED 171 331)

118

Sadler, W. A., Jr. "Tapping the Potentials of Interdisciplinary Studies in a Freshman Core Program." Unpublished paper, 1978. 16 pp. (ED 167 231)

Sanborn, D. H. "Why All CCC Students Need General Education: A Position Paper in Support of Resolutions Proposed by the City Colleges Study Group." Prepared for the "Education: Planning for the Quality 1980s" Conference, Chicago, Illinois, November 30–December 1, 1979. 21 pp. (ED 180 519)

Shaw, R. G. "General Education in the DCCCD (Dallas County Community College District) and Skills for Living." Paper presented at the 61st Annual Convention of the American Association of Community and Junior Colleges, Washington, D.C., April 20–22, 1981. 22 pp. (ED 203 913)

Strasser, W. C. *For the Community: Continuing General Education. Community Colleges and General Education: Three Perspectives. Part 3.* Rockville, Md.: Montgomery College, 1979. 144 pp. (ED 172 846)

Tighe, D. J. (Ed.) *Poet on the Moon: A Dialogue on Liberal Education in the Community College.* Washington, D.C.: Association of American Colleges, 1977. 21 pp. (ED 145 870; Available in microfiche only)

Walker, N. "Institutional Change Through Defining Competencies." Paper presented to the Florida Association of Community Colleges, Orlando, Florida, November 14, 1980. 24 pp. (ED 198 879)

James C. Palmer is the user-services librarian at the ERIC Clearinghouse for Junior Colleges, University of California at Los Angeles.

Index

Statement of Ownership , Management, and Circulation
(Required by 39 U.S.C. 3685)

1. Title of Publication: New Directions for Community Colleges. A. Publication number: USPS 121-710. 2. Date of filing: 9/30/82. 3. Frequency of issue: quarterly. A. Number of issues published annually: four. B. Annual subscription price: $35 institutions; $21 individuals. 4. Location of known office of publication: 433 California Street, San Francisco (San Francisco County), California 94104. 5. Location of the headquarters or general business offices of the publishers: 433 California Street, San Francisco (San Francisco County), California 94104. 6. Names and addresses of publisher, editor, and managing editor: publisher—Jossey-Bass Inc., Publishers, 433 California Street, San Francisco, California 94104; editor—Arthur Cohen, ERIC, 96 Powell Library Bldg., UCLA, Los Angeles, CA 90024; managing editor—Allen Jossey-Bass, 433 California Street, San Francisco, California 94104. 7. Owner: Jossey-Bass Inc., Publishers, 433 California Street, San Francisco, California 94104. 8. Known bondholders, mortgages, and other security holders owning or holding 1 percent or more of total amount of bonds, mortgages, or other securities: same as No. 7. 10. Extent and nature of circulation: (Note: first number indicates average number of copies of each issue during the preceding 12 months; the second number indicates the actual number of copies published nearest to filing date.) A. Total number of copies printed (net press run): 2667, 1996. B. Paid circulation, 1) Sales through dealers and carriers, street vendors, and counter sales: 85, 40. 2) Mail subscriptions: 975, 908. C. Total paid circulation: 1060, 948. D. Free distribution by mail, carrier, or other means (samples, complimentary, and other free copies): 275, 275. E. Total distribution (sum of C and D): 1335, 1223. F. Copies not distributed, 1) Office use, left over, unaccounted, spoiled after printing: 1332, 773. 2) Returns from news agents: 0, 0. G. Total (sum of E, F1, and 2—should equal net press run shown in A): 2667, 1996. I certify that the statements made by me above are correct and complete.

JOHN R. WARD
Vice-President